D0438459

THE
ZULU WAR

GREAT BATTLES OF HISTORY

Hanson W. Baldwin, GENERAL EDITOR

Also by Rupert Furneaux

THE BREAKFAST WAR (The Siege of Plevna)

THE
ZULU WAR:

Isandhlwana and Rorke's Drift

RUPERT FURNEAUX

J. B. LIPPINCOTT COMPANY
Philadelphia & New York

The maps of Isandhlwana and Rorke's Drift are based on originals drawn by Major Archie Savory.

CONTENTS

MAPS

THE
ZULU WAR

1

SHAKA'S WARNING

"I HEAR THE SOUND of the feet of a great white people. They will tread this land flat." These were the strange, prophetic last words spoken by Shaka, the Great King of the Zulus, after he was fatally stabbed by his jealous brothers. The date was September 28, 1828. By "white people" Shaka meant the British, the only whites the Zulus then knew.

For fifty years Shaka's successors kept an uneasy peace with the British in South Africa. His brother Dingaan defeated the invading Boers, rapacious for his lands, and his brother Panda held off both the British and the Dutch farmers who were pressing in on the Zulu frontier. Then in 1879, during the reign of his son Cetewayo, the British invaded Zululand. Without provocation and with no legitimate excuse, a British army crossed the frontier and marched on Ulundi, Cetewayo's capital. Reluctantly the Zulu king launched his impis to defend the land from those whom he had believed to be his friends.

This is the story of the clash between Cetewayo's savage warriors and the soldiers of the Great White Queen over the water, one armed with weapons that had been outdated for a thousand years and the other equipped with the latest death-dealing inventions of a great industrial nation. At Isandhlwana, Rorke's Drift, Kambula and Ulundi, the forces of "Roman" and "modern" times locked in battle. The outcome was inevitable, of course, but not before the swift Zulus had inflicted a terrible defeat on the British—a defeat that must rank with the most glorious failures in British military history.

The story of the British massacre at Isandhlwana belongs in the great tradition of Balaklava, Mons and Dunkirk. The gallant defence of Rorke's Drift ranks with the epic of Thermopylae. As military or political events these two battles had not the slightest significance. They were but episodes in war, as purposeless as the charge of the Light Brigade. They are worthy of our memory for other reasons: beneath that little hill and by that narrow stream in faraway Zululand there met in combat two great peoples who should by all rights have been friends. Mutual respect demanded it; self-interest dictated it. Yet soldier lads from the pasture lands of rural Warwickshire and from the dusty kraals of Zululand met in a clash in which, surprised and unprepared, the overwhelmed British died by the hundreds; and, mowed down by bullets and shrapnel, the Zulu boys were slain by the thousands. The survivors of each side—a mere handful of British and the decimated Zulu army—left the scene of conflict with only admiration for the prowess and bravery of the other.

The story of the battle of Isandhlwana and the defence of Rorke's Drift is the story of men at war: men, white and black, who fought bravely and died gloriously for something few of them understood, and that in the year 1879 few white people understood. Perhaps we, in the perspective afforded by the passage of over eighty years, can better understand it.

The Zulu people in 1879 were in the way. The Natal

[4]

colonists regarded the Zulu army as a constant menace to their security. At any moment, they believed, Cetewayo might send his black impis ravaging and burning, slaying and slaughtering, amongst his white neighbours. Better to scotch the dangerous snake before it could strike. The Dutch farmers of the Transvaal, the descendants of the Boer trekkers who had crossed swords with Dingaan, desired the land of the Zulus, who, credulous and naïve, were fair game for the hard-faced diplomacy of Pietermaritzburg, Pretoria, Cape Town and London.

But *were* the Zulus poised to strike? The evidence is against it. If King Cetewayo was the black despot he was made out to be by frightened missionaries, and if he had been planning to invade Natal in 1879, why, then, did the victorious British put him back on his throne in 1883?

To understand the events that led up to the wanton British attack, we must flick back the pages of the history of South Africa—the tip of the continent the Phoenicians rounded, the Portuguese discovered, the Dutch settled and the British seized, to relinquish to men who would try to turn back the hands of time.

2

BOER AND ZULU

THE DUTCH had been settled on the Cape of Good Hope for 154 years when the British captured Cape Town in 1806, during the Napoleonic Wars. British control was bitterly resented by the Boers, who, finally exasperated by the abolition of slavery—the system by which they ran their farms—packed up and trekked northwards to find a land where they could live their lives in their own way, not subject to British meddling.

The Great Trek, the famous exodus of the Boers from Cape Colony, started in 1835. It occurred at the same time that a vast number of the Bantu peoples were surging southwards, pushed by the conquests of the Zulu king Shaka. The Bantus had been moving down east Africa for 500 years. A virile, prolific race, they clashed head on with South Africa's white migrants over possession of Africa's fairest lands: a vast area of plains (which the Dutch called the "veldt"), high mountains, deep valleys and swift-flowing rivers that in time was to prove incalculably rich in mineral wealth.

The Zulus themselves, one tiny Bantu clan, reached southeast Africa in the eighteenth century. They had not been there

when Vasco da Gama discovered and named Natal on Christ-
mas Day, 1497, nor in 1687, when a group of shipwrecked
Dutch and English mariners penetrated inland for 150 miles.
In 1816, the year after Napoleon's defeat at Waterloo, Shaka
embarked on the conquest of the neighbouring tribes; by 1823
he was overlord of an area of 100,000 square miles, stretching
from the Limpopo River in the north to the borders of Cape
Colony on the south. He achieved his victories by military
genius and consolidated his gains by rare organising ability. As
he wiped out the tribes that dared to oppose him, he enrolled
their men in his army and their women in his kraals. He en-
forced iron discipline and demanded unflinching bravery, himself setting the example. Weaklings were slaughtered; the
disobedient were put to death. A man who broke the line in
combat was killed. By white standards Shaka was cruel, savage
and ruthless. But under his rule the Zulu became the most
powerful native race in South Africa, rich, prosperous and
feared. Like the Romans long before them, the Zulus con-
quered their known world. Sooner or later they were certain
to clash with the whites now moving slowly northwards.
That was as inevitable as the battles on the American frontier
between the Indians and the westward-moving pioneers. In the
long run the result was just as inevitable, for the discovery of
gunpowder had made the Europeans the most powerful peoples in the world, and enabled the few to conquer the many.

In 1824 Shaka welcomed two English visitors, Lieutenant
Farewell and Henry Francis Fynn. Shaka liked the English
and, thinking there was much to be learned from them, was
anxious to establish cordial relations with the "people of
George" (the fourth British king of that name). Toward this
end, he ceded the port of Durban to the British for use as a
centre of trade.

[7]

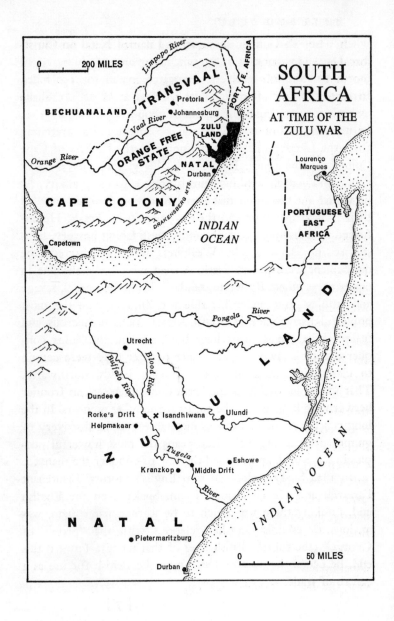

SOUTH
AFRICA

AT TIME OF THE
ZULU WAR

In 1828 Shaka was assassinated. He was succeeded by his brother and murderer, Dingaan, who withdrew the Zulus north of the Tugela River, leaving Natal unoccupied. This attracted British colonists, whose occupation of Natal Dingaan recognised in a treaty concluded in 1835. One clause of the treaty read as follows:

> The British residents at Port Natal [Durban] engage for the future never to receive or harbour any deserter from the Zulu country, and to use every endeavour to secure the return to the king of every individual trying to find an asylum among them.

Meanwhile, the emigrant Boers had trekked northwards in their lumbering wagons to the area that was to become the Orange Free State, the northeastern part of which was separated from Natal by the natural barrier of the Drakensberg Mountains, and to the area beyond the Vaal River (the Transvaal), whose ill-defined southern frontier bordered on Zululand. For this "high veldt" the Boers had to fight the Basutos and Matabeles. How a few hundred Boers quickly vanquished these warlike peoples has considerable bearing on our story.

Durable, courageous and ever alert, the Boers were extremely effective in native warfare. In combat each man was a self-contained unit, carrying his own food, water and ammunition. Each man was expert at firing from the saddle at a moving target, and in open country Boer commandos would ride up to within rifle range, discharge their muskets, then retreat to reload. They would repeat this procedure until the enemy, discouraged by its losses and its inability to bring the Boers to close quarters, withdrew.

Especially adept at defence, the Boers kept patrols out covering a wide area to guard against surprise attacks. Whenever the Boers travelled by wagon train, at night or at the approach of an enemy each wagon would be chained to the one next to it to form a circle that enclosed the Boers and their livestock. If an attack occurred, a withering barrage was kept up from within the laager until the natives, who usually vastly outnumbered the defenders, were routed.

The first tribe the Boer trekkers met, the Basutos, were crushed in a series of minor encounters. The Matabeles, the people of Mosilikatzi, one of Shaka's generals, were tougher opponents, caught as they were between two fires: in the rear their Zulu cousins, and in front the Boers seeking pasture land. At Vegkop, on the Vaal River in 1836, 5,000 Matabeles threw themselves on a train of twenty Boer wagons. All day long they attacked the circle of wagons. From dawn till dusk the tiny force of defenders poured a leaden hail into the enemy's charging ranks. Two thousand Matabeles lost their lives outside the Boer wagons; inside the magic circle only two Boers were killed.

But the Matabele nation was still a menace to Boer security; they had to be wiped out before the scattered Boer farms would be safe. In 1837 a commando surprised and attacked the chief Matabele kraal; the enemy was dispersed but was still dangerous. Another commando caught the Matabele impis on the high veldt, defeating them after days of running combat. Mosilikatzi had had enough; he led his people away to the north of the Limpopo River, to the future Rhodesia, where they were finally destroyed in 1896.

From their conquests the Boers founded the Orange Free State and the Transvaal Republic. But these broad acres of arid land provided only a few large farms, at a time when each Boer family could do with no less than 12,000 acres. The land-hungry Boers looked eastward to Natal, rich in land, well watered and abounding in game. In 1837 a great fleet of Boer wagons lumbered over the Drakensbergs. The leader, Piet Retief, went boldly to the Zulu king, Dingaan, requesting permission to settle. Squatting on his royal kaross of leopard skins, surrounded by his indunas, Dingaan pondered. His subtle and treacherous mind worked quickly. Behind Retief, he knew, were a thousand moving wagons—the forerunners of the dangerous Boers who had wiped out Mosilikatzi, a general for whom Dingaan had the utmost respect.

Dingaan lacked Shaka's genius. Cunning, cruel, and avaricious, he could think only of immediate advantage. By promising them land he would get the Boers to do a piece of dirty work for him; once this had been done, the unsuspecting Boers would be wiped out. A foolhardy chief named Sikonyela had stolen 500 head of Dingaan's cattle, an unpardonable crime that meant a severe loss to the royal herd. To storm Sikonyela's kraal nestled high in the Drakensbergs would cost many Zulu lives and cost the royal exchequer many more fat cattle to feed the impi.

If the Boers would get his cattle back and teach Sikonyela a lesson, Dingaan told Retief, they would get the land they desired. Retief set out at the head of a commando. On the way he met the Boer wagons, now spreading out along the streams that poured down the empty foothills.

When, in January, 1838, Retief returned to Dingaan's kraal at Umgungindhlovu, behind him were the stolen cattle, and with him the sixty-eight Boers who had helped him to recover them. Retief claimed as fulfillment of the contract the promised land, which Dingaan had no intention of giving in payment.

Those who have read H. Rider Haggard's novel *Marie*, written fifty years after the event, will recall his reconstruction of Dingaan's treachery. The Boers were regaled by the apparently friendly Zulu king. February 6, 1838, was the day

[11]

for the signing of the deed of gift. Dingaan invited his guests to the cattle kraal for a dancing display by his regiments. Protocol demanded that the Boers leave their guns behind; to appear armed in the royal presence was unlawful. Also, the carrying of weapons would show suspicion, the Boers were urged. They had nothing to fear; Dingaan's intentions were honorable, declared Retief. Their weapons left stacked by the gate, the Boers grouped themselves round the Zulu king. Native beer and food were served. Hour after hour the regiments danced. At last Retief rose to take his leave. His signature and Dingaan's mark were affixed to the deed. Dingaan withdrew to the gate of his private huts. Drawing his kaross over his eyes, he turned; "Slay the wizards," he ordered. A thousand warriors flung themselves upon the Boers, who very quickly were dragged away to the Hill of Slaughter, over which the Asvogels, the scavaging vultures of Zululand, hovered daily in expectancy of a feast. Sixty-nine Boers—all who attended the signing—were killed.

An impi rushed out to slay the Boer families, who, incautiously relying on the promises of the Zulu king, were settling themselves in the land, now and forever after to be known as "The Land of Weeping"—Weenen. Taken unawares at night, scattered and unsuspecting, the Boer husbands and fathers had time to fire only a few shots. Forty-one of them were killed, 280 of their women and children put to the assegai. The survivors fled back over the Drakensbergs.

In their eagerness to avenge their comrades' death, the Boers threw to the winds the caution that had helped them win the Transvaal. At Italeni one commando was caught by a Zulu impi in rough country on ground too broken for manoeuvre. The indomitable Boers fought their way out of the trap, the majority getting away. But they had been beaten by

the Zulus, and their leader, Piet Uys, had been killed. Emboldened by his triumph, Dingaan launched another impi
against British settlers in Durban. Warned of its approach,
they escaped on shipboard, watching from afar for nine days
while the Zulus ravaged their settlement. Another group of
settlers, forming a laager in time, drove the Zulus off.

The Boers refused to give up Natal. Andries Pretorius,
their greatest leader, himself came to teach the Zulu king a
lesson. With a commando 500 strong he entered Zululand; on
the banks of the Buffalo River, he drew up his wagons into a
laager and awaited the Zulu attack. On January 2, 1840, the
Zulu warriors, the regiments trained by Shaka, flung themselves for six hours against the impenetrable circle. Thousands
died. The Zulus hesitated, never before having experienced
such heavy gunfire. Seizing their opportunity, the Boers rode
out and drove a wedge into the wavering ranks, pushing the
Zulus down the banks of the river, soon a pool of blood. The
"Battle of the Blood River" it came to be called by both
Zulus and Boers.

By the time the Boers reached the Zulu capital, Dingaan
had fled. On the Hill of Slaughter, they found the skeletons
of Retief and his men, picked clean by the vultures. In Retief's
haversack was the deed of cession, undamaged and still valid.
Once again the Boer wagons lumbered over the Drakensbergs.
But as long as Dingaan ruled the Zulus, the Boers felt inse-
cure. They learned that his brother Panda was planning a
revolt; secret messages were exchanged. Panda and Pretorius
agreed to act together to rid Zululand and Natal of the
treacherous Dingaan. Supported by a Boer commando, Panda
defeated Dingaan, who fled and was soon murdered.

The good-natured Panda now ruled in Zululand. The Boers
settled in Natal, forming an independent republic like that of

their brothers in the Transvaal and Orange Free State. But they had reckoned without the British. Determined to retain their colony of Natal, the Cape government sent troops to Durban. After several clashes, the Boers submitted, and a treaty was made between the Government of Natal and Panda, defining the Zulu frontier on the Tugela River. Peace reigned in Natal, and throughout South Africa. By the Sand River Convention of 1852, the British recognised the right of the Boers of the Orange Free State and of the Transvaal to manage their own affairs and govern themselves without interference, according to their own laws.

In Zululand Panda's sons, Cetewayo and Umbulazi, fought for the succession; in 1856 Cetewayo defeated his brother in a bloody battle and became the heir to the throne. In 1861 Theophilus Shepstone, the Secretary for Native Affairs in Natal, came to Zululand and recognised Cetewayo as Panda's successor. When the old king died in 1873, Shepstone returned to attend Cetewayo's coronation as a mark of respect. He took the opportunity to secure from the new king certain promises, in the form of the following four principles by which his country would be ruled:

1. That the indiscriminate shedding of blood would cease.

2. That no Zulu would be condemned without open trial, and without public examination of all witnesses; and that each convicted man would have the right of appeal to the king.

3. That, once a trial had taken place and the right of appeal had been exercised, no Zulu life would be taken without the knowledge and consent of the king.

4. And that for minor crimes the loss of property, all or a portion of it, would be substituted for the death penalty.

Cetewayo's failure to keep these "promises" became one of the excuses for the British invasion of Zululand six years later.

Cetewayo, son of Panda and nephew of the great Shaka, was left to rule his people, 250,000 strong, rich in cattle, contented and prosperous after thirty-two years of peace. Prophet, priest and king, an efficient rain maker and driver out of evil spirits, Cetewayo was popular with his people, who, cheerful and happy in their well-ordered existence, grouped together in their scattered kraals—the men building and maintaining the huts and herding the cattle, the women, several wives to each man, tilling the soil and doing the domestic work. Children were loved, but were brought up in strict discipline and taught good manners, sobriety, honesty and morality. Adultery was punished by death, but a form of restricted love-making between youths and maidens was permitted.

In the middle of the nineteenth century, the Zulus were a noble race, refined and brave. But they were the victims of two dangerous national habits: superstition and militarism. They believed in evil spirits who had to be propitiated by magic and could only be exorcized by the death of the person they possessed. Fear of the witch doctors pervaded the land; every man, particularly if he were rich in cattle, might be "smelt out" as a harbourer of evil spirits, dangerous to his neighbours, and put to death with all his house. The Zulu army, created by Shaka to make his people great, had grown into a Frankenstein's monster. The youth of the nation were drafted into regiments according to age groups. Abandoning home and family, they lived celibate in military kraals, minding the king's cattle and acting as the national police force while drilling for war. No young soldier was allowed to marry without permission of the king, who seldom granted it until the soldier was nearly forty years of age, or until he had killed an enemy in battle, when by national custom he could request the privilege of restrained sexual intercourse with any girl he met. The army was his career, and war afforded the only chance he ever got to gain honour and cattle. Not unnaturally the Zulu army clamoured for war. Cetewayo put them off with excuses, but the pressure increased; for militarism was as much a part of the Zulus' national life as religion was of the Jews'. War and life were inseparable. Sooner or later, the Zulu army, exultant in its manhood but frustrated by inactivity, would prove a stumbling block to peace.

3

THE BARBARIAN
DESPOT

Was zulu militarism a standing menace to their white neighbours? One man in South Africa feared that at any moment Cetewayo might launch his "celibate man-slaying machine" on Natal. It became his obsession, and was his principal excuse for invading Zululand in January 1879.

Sir Bartle Frere arrived in South Africa to take up his appointment as Governor General of Cape Colony and High Commissioner of Natal early in 1877. His powers were wide; he came on his own terms. He had had a long and distinguished career in India. Aged sixty-two, a veteran of the Sepoy Mutiny, he had been Governor of Bombay, a member of the Governor General's Council, and, on his return to England, had served on the Indian Council. He had proved himself a great proconsul, accustomed and expecting to decide matters for himself. Success had made him confident; it may even have gone to his head. It is possible that Frere saw himself as a new Clive, another Wolfe, adding a fresh jewel to Queen Victoria's crown, a great South African empire.

Frere was confident he could solve South Africa's problems: the antagonism of British and Boers, the condition of natives under Boer rule, and the Zulu menace. These potentially dangerous situations could be overcome only by the unification of South Africa under a strong central government, in which all whites would co-operate and by which the native races could be protected and controlled.

Frere saw South Africa as a grumbling volcano that might erupt at any moment. While he believed that the Boers and British could be made to sink their differences and curb their jealousies, he was obsessed with the Zulu danger. To Frere Cetewayo was a treacherous despot, irresponsible, bloodthirsty. His warriors thought themselves invincible. The situation was explosive: 350,000 whites, under two separate and mutually hostile governments, lived amongst and surrounded by 3,000,000 natives. Only a spark was needed for South Africa to explode in violence.

Early in 1877 Sir Theophilus Shepstone was sent to Pretoria to annex the Transvaal to the British Crown. Several cogent reasons dictated this fundamental change in British policy. The Boers had suffered a humiliating defeat at the hands of a native chieftain; they were trespassing on Zulu territory, seizing land that did not belong to them—acts that might at any moment precipitate a war; their treatment of their own native population was disgraceful; and the Transvaal Republic was bankrupt. It had incurred debts of £300,000 and there was only twelve shillings and sixpence in the treasury. Trade was paralysed and the ordinary functions of government had ceased. The Boer dream of a great anti-British confederacy was over, at least for a time.

Shepstone's arrival in Pretoria brought instant response from Cetewayo, who massed his regiments on the Transvaal border, to protect his friend Sometsu, he said. Shepstone ordered him to withdraw, warning Cetewayo that the Transvaal was now British territory. Cetewayo withdrew at once, plaintively begging Shepstone to allow him "one little raid, one small swoop." It was the custom of his country, he told Shepstone, when a new king came to the throne for the nation to "wash its spears," and there had been no fighting since he came to the throne. "I am no king. I sit in a heap," Cetewayo complained to "his father Sometsu."

By annexing the Transvaal the British upset the balance of power in South Africa, as they had done in 1759 in North America by defeating the French, thus freeing the colonists from the fear of outside aggression. No longer could the Boers and Zulus be played off against each other, and the Zulus were now surrounded by British territory. If they wanted war, the British were the only people they could attack, a danger that would not be removed, Frere believed, "until they had tried their strength against us and learnt by sad experience." The Zulus had to be thoroughly convinced of "our superior power," he told the Colonial Secretary, Sir Michael Hicks-Beach, in London.

Sir Bartle Frere moved his headquarters from the Cape to Pietermaritzburg in Natal. He was determined to draw Cetewayo's teeth, to crush him before he could strike at Natal. Frere believed that only by striking first could he save the colony from the horrors of a Zulu raid and rescue the Zulu people from Cetewayo's oppression. Frere believed that the Zulu army was a constant danger. He claimed that Cetewayo was trying to organise a general rising of natives against the whites throughout South Africa. He declared that Cetewayo's indiscriminate killing of his own subjects without trial was a breach of his coronation promises.

By the annexation of the Transvaal the British had inherited the long-standing boundary disputes between the Boers and Zulus. In 1875 Boer freebooters had crossed the Pongola River and annexed a stretch of land. With exemplary patience Cetewayo agreed to allow the Government of Natal to settle the vexing question of this disputed territory. The Boers, he claimed, having first been given leave by a local chief to graze cattle, put up a shanty and then a house. More and more Boers came, like toads hopping and hopping, until at last they hopped into the middle. The situation, Frere saw, was critical, for neither side would yield, and a race war could be precipitated at any moment. He appointed a commission to settle the dispute. To his surprise it decided that the disputed territory belonged to the Zulus. The award infuriated the Boers and put Frere in an awkward position, for the protection of the Boers from the Zulus had been the chief justification for the annexation of the Transvaal. Frere determined to make the acceptance of the award by the Zulus conditional on their promise to disband their army, which was no longer necessary, Frere told Cetewayo. He was now surrounded only by friends, by British territories.

Frere distrusted Cetewayo. The award, he believed, might be interpreted by him as an admission of weakness. He kept its terms secret and ordered Lord Chelmsford, newly appointed commander of the British forces in South Africa, to move his troops up from Cape Colony, where he had recently crushed a Kaffir rebellion, to Natal, to reinforce the small British garrison. "It is quite clear that the war spirit is abroad," Frere wrote to the Colonial Secretary in London in June 1878. The Zulus meant mischief, he stated, declaring, "The sooner the root of the evil, which I consider to be the Zulu power and military organisation, is dealt with, the easier our task will be."

The Zulus made no move to threaten Natal, but in minor ways they irritated the British, providing Frere with trivial excuses to bring matters to a head.

In July, the Zulus violated the Natal frontier. Ka Qwelebana, wife of the old man Sirayo (one of Cetewayo's chiefs), a self-confessed adulteress, eloped with her young lover to Natal, where she took refuge in the hut of a border guard. Sirayo's sons crossed the Tugela River in pursuit. Early next morning the guard heard the sound of horses approaching, and coming out of his hut he found himself surrounded by nearly forty men, commanded by Sirayo's son Mehlokazulu. Another fifty men or so, armed with assegais, came up from the rear. The hut was searched, Ka Qwelebana dragged out, "as if she had been an old hide," in the border guard's words, and taken back over the river to be killed. Another wife suffered similar treatment. Sir Henry Bulwer, the Governor of Natal, demanded the surrender of the frontier violators within twenty days and the payment of a fine of 500 cattle. Cetewayo offered his apologies and £50, calling the incident "the rash act of boys in the zeal of their father's house." He pointed out that adultery was a crime punishable by death in Zululand, and he referred to the treaty concluded with Dingaan in 1835 whereby the British in Natal engaged never to harbour deserters from Zululand, and to secure their return. When Bulwer seemed inclined to accept Cetewayo's offer, Frere told him, "It is necessary to send an ultimatum which must necessarily put an end to pacific relations with our neighbors."

Another frontier incident occurred in October. Two Natal government surveyors named Smith and Deighton were seized by the Zulus as they were inspecting the middle drift across the Tugela, clearly, the Zulus said, examining the ford for purposes of invasion. To British protests Cetewayo pointed out politely that the two surveyors had been found on Zulu territory, on two islands on the Zulu side of the river, as the Governor of Natal would learn if he sent someone to inspect the place.

About this time, too, in the waning South African winter of 1878, a number of disgruntled British, German and Norwegian missionaries who had been trying vainly since 1866 to bring the Zulus to the light, returned to Natal, claiming that the Zulu people were groaning under the oppression of a tyrannous king who killed to satisfy caprice or cupidity, and demanding that the "godless despot" be overthrown. "Heathenism must perish. God wills it so," angrily declared the Reverend P. D. Heppburn. "We have the approbation of God, our Queen and our conscience," stormed another missionary. They cited a number of examples of Cetewayo's cruelty, including the killing of a vast number, hundreds or even thousands, they declared, of young girls who had evaded the king's command to marry the men of one of his older regiments. To remain faithful to their lovers, the men of a younger regiment, these girls had conceived the ingenious idea of getting themselves adopted as extra wives, in name only, by their lovers' elder brothers.

Frere fully accepted these missionary tales. "An unparalleled act of barbarity," he called the killing of the girls. The matter was put into better perspective by Mr. Osborne, a frontier magistrate, who reported that "several" girls had been killed. Frere declared that Cetewayo had, throughout his reign, violated his "coronation promises"—agreements on the king's part that were magnified by the British into solemn promises of new legislation—by killing people without trial.

[22]

Cetewayo replied that his people would ignore the laws except under penalty of death. The Zulus believed in witchcraft, and, in killing those possessed by evil spirits that might bewitch others, he was only protecting his people. It was the custom of his people, he told Frere, and he did not intend to depart from it. He wished to be friends with the British, he said, but the Government of Natal had no right to dictate how he should rule his country. "I do not go to Natal and dictate to the Governor about his laws," Cetewayo complained. "Go back and tell the Governor of Natal that he and I are equal," he told Shepstone. "He is the Governor of Natal, and I am the Governor here."

Cetewayo's alleged ill-treatment of his own subjects was one of Frere's major excuses for coercing his black neighbours. Bishop Colenso of Natal, the most fanatical friend of the black man, although he agreed with Frere that the Zulu standing army was a menace, believed that Cetewayo wished to remain friendly with the British and to avoid war unless it was forced upon him.

Frere never met Cetewayo. He had no firsthand contact with the Zulus. His beliefs were based on hearsay. As the year 1878 advanced, the opinions he voiced of Cetewayo became more violent, his acts more aggressive, his whipping up of the colonists' fears more determined. He spoke of Cetewayo's "grinding despotism," "his atrocious barbarity," "his faithless and cruel character"; he called him an "irresponsible, bloodthirsty and treacherous despot," and declared that "his highest aspiration was to emulate Shaka."

On September 23, Frere wrote to Sir Michael Hicks-Beach:

> The Zulus are quite out of hand, and the maintenance of peace depends upon their forbearance. I speak with a deep

sense of responsibility for what I say, when I assure you that the peace of South Africa for many years to come seems to me to depend on your taking steps to put a final end to Zulu pretensions to dictate to Her Majesty's Government what they may or may not do to protect their colonies in South Africa, and that unless you settle with the Zulus you will find it difficult, if not impossible, to govern the Transvaal without a considerable standing force of troops.

On the same day he told the Colonial Under Secretary, "There is no lack of prophets of peace hereabouts, but I feel convinced that the Zulus are boiling over with warlike conceit and will not let us alone"; and he reminded him that it was the Zulu practice to attack suddenly and without warning, relying on white unpreparedness and their own discipline.

It was Cetewayo's avowed policy to recover the position held by Shaka, Frere told his superiors in London. To the Colonial Secretary he wrote on December 2:

I would not for an instant question our responsibility for putting an end to a system which locks up all the manhood of the country in a compulsory celibacy, considered by the despot necessary to the efficiency of his army, that army having no possible use but to threaten us or other friendly people who surround him, a system which massacres by hundreds the young women who refuse at his bidding to become the wives of the elderly soldiers to whom they are told off, a system which destroys all private property and industry, which forbids all improvements by civilisation or education, and relies solely on a regular course of murder and plunder by armed bands of the King's soldiers for the replenishment of the royal exchequer.

"Our right to interfere, to compel Cetewayo to govern as well as a good and respectable native ruler can govern, rests on the first law of nature, the instinct of self-preservation," Frere stated. He asked for reinforcements to prevent a "war of races," and pointed out that on the other side of a fordable river "stood the Zulu army, forty to sixty thousand strong, well armed, unconquered, insolent, burning to clear out the white man." Natal owed its immunity to the "irresolution of a conceited savage," he told the Colonial Secretary. "Anxiety to try conclusions with the white man pervades the whole mass of the Zulus," he declared.

Up to this time the Imperial Government had supported Frere. "Cetewayo must be kept in order," they instructed him. But now it suddenly reversed its policy. The reinforcements Frere had asked for could not be sent, he was told, the government expressing its "confident hope that by the exercise of prudence and by meeting the Zulus in a spirit of forbearance and reasonable compromise, it would be possible to avert the very serious evil of war with Cetewayo."

The refusal of reinforcements for South Africa was due to the situation in Europe, where there was fear of war with Russia, and on the Northwest frontier of India, where Afghanistan was in revolt. The Imperial Government was "most anxious" to avoid war with Cetewayo, Frere was instructed.

The Imperial Government's veto on a war with the Zulus came two days too late. Frere had already decided to finally settle the Zulu problem. On December 8 he instructed Cetewayo to send his councillors to the frontier to receive the decision of the Boundary Commission. With it he intended to serve Cetewayo with an ultimatum.

Cetewayo watched the military preparations in Natal with anxiety. He heard rumours of the enrollment of volunteers, the formation of three native regiments and the arrival of British regiments equipped with twenty cannon. He felt himself surrounded, he told border agent Bernard Fynney. The Queen of England, he had heard, had given orders that he should be bound and brought before her, and he intended to take steps to protect himself and his country, he said.

Cetewayo had good cause to fear British aggression, more reason than had Frere to fear Zulu aggression. For thirty years the Zulus and the Natal colonists had lived side by side, separated only by a narrow river, in peaceful enmity. But Frere was determined to launch a preventive war, to strike first. He made a demand that he knew Cetewayo would not and could not accept. He ordered that the Zulu army be disbanded, to be mobilised again only with the consent of the British. Cetewayo must receive a British Resident at his capital, Frere stated in the ultimatum which was presented to Cetewayo's indunas, his councillors, on December 11. First the boundary award was read to them. Their lands were to be returned to them in name only, and the Zulus were forbidden to occupy them. Then the ultimatum was read, and Cetewayo's councillors were told that the king had twenty days to satisfy its terms, which included the surrender of Sirayo's sons and the payment of the fine of 500 cattle.

The terms of the ultimatum were brought to Cetewayo on December 21. He ordered the cattle to be rounded up, but he refused to give up Mehlokazulu and his brothers, or to disband his army. He refused to yield to threats, he told his councillors. His request for an extension of time was turned down. Frere called it a "pitiful evasion" and insisted on "rigid punctuality." Lord Chelmsford was ordered to move his troops to the Zulu border.

On January 4, 1879, Frere, declaring he had "exhausted all peaceful means," issued a formal notification of Cetewayo's default. Unless unqualified and complete acceptance of the

British terms was offered by January 11, the British army would invade Zululand, Cetewayo was informed. At the same time the Zulu people were told that the British government had no quarrel with them.

Frere wrote to the Colonial Secretary, telling him, "Cetewayo's arrogance has increased." A "final settlement" was now inevitable, and he hoped for a speedy and complete crushing of the Zulu military system. "Of the perfect justice of our cause, I think you can have no doubt," Frere assured him, and "by God's help we can relieve South Africa of the Zulu incubus." He referred to Cetewayo's "thousands of young gladiators, so irresistible when they believe themselves invincible." "Their courage," he confidently assured the Colonial Secretary, "is the courage of maniacs and drunkards, of wild beasts, infuriated and trained to destruction, and once cowed they will not rally."

Frere's twenty-day ultimatum to a savage king was an act of war. The Zulu army was a national institution that could not be disbanded by a stroke of the pen, as Frere well knew. Every man between the ages of sixteen and sixty was a trained soldier, needing only a call to arms to seize his assegai and a bag of mealies (the native name for Indian corn) and join his regiment. The Zulu impis could be rendered harmless only by their destruction in war, which, Frere fervently believed, was the only way to protect the Natal colonists from the terrible threat of Zulu aggression.

Was Cetewayo preparing to launch his "celibate man-slaying machine" on the defenceless colonists of Natal, as Frere thought? It does not look as if he was. Given a golden opportunity a few weeks later, he refused to allow his impis to cross the frontier.

4

MILITARY
PREPARATIONS

Lord chelmsford stood ready on the Zulu frontier. For months he and Frere had discussed the invasion of Zululand —the "promenade" through Zululand, as it was confidently expected to be. Volunteer mounted corps had been raised amongst the colonists; three native regiments had been en-rolled; wagons, oxen, mules and horses purchased; food, fod-der and ammunition collected. Under his command Chelmsford had 17,929 officers and men, six thousand of them British or of European descent. Twenty cannon, fieldpieces throwing seven-pound shells, had been brought from England. This made for a ponderous, slow-moving, cumbersome force with which to cross a wild country that was completely lacking in roads and that had been waterlogged by the summer rains—a country thick in forests, crisscrossed by swift-flowing rivers, rugged mountains, narrow valleys, dark ravines and countless small water-courses and crevasses. Rough ground perfect for concealment, every mile progressed in it was another mile in which to move supplies and to protect communications.

Lord Chelmsford's army was not as strong as it looked on paper. Its weakness lay in its native troops, who were so mistrusted that only one man in ten was armed with a gun, the rest carrying their traditional assegais and shields. Zulus of a sort, inhabitants of Natal, they were commanded by colonists with little experience of war, and by noncommissioned officers, "old soldiers" who could keep up with neither their officers on horseback nor the nimble natives. Many of these white sergeants and corporals were of poor character; the only prerequisite for enrollment was service in the regular army, and the natives had no respect for these men. A mistake also was made in attempting European drill and organisation instead of allowing the men to fight under their tribal leaders. Under their own headmen these native troops could have been successfully employed as scouts and skirmishers. But no one should have expected them to stand the shock of pitched battle.

The British troops were of good quality, but the regiments of the line were in part composed of beardless boys who, under the Army Act of 1870, had replaced veterans of long service—men who, twenty-five years before, had stood up to the charging Russian cavalry at Balaklava and stormed the Redan and Malakoff forts of Sebastopol. Before the Zulu campaign opened Lord Chelmsford had found it necessary to complain to the Commander in Chief, the Duke of Cambridge, in London that a large proportion of the draftees he had received were recently recruited and untrained in the elementary principles of drill and musketry. Nonetheless these young men fought like veterans.

The British infantry consisted of the 1st and 2nd Battalions of the 24th Foot—the Warwickshire Regiment—and a number of companies drawn from the 3rd, 56th, 80th, 90th and 99th Regiments. Each soldier was equipped with a Martini–Henry hammerless, single-shot, breech-loading rifle whose ejector worked by means of a lever placed behind the trigger guard. Fitted to carry a bayonet, the rifle was sighted to 1,000 yards and fired a heavy bullet of great stopping power, propelled by a charge of black powder.

With a few modifications the soldiers' uniform was the same as that of Crimean days. Each man wore a red jacket, blue trousers, white leather belt and shoulder straps, heavy boots and a helmet; and each man carried an ammunition pouch capable of containing seventy rounds, in addition to a water bottle and haversack. The officers wore red or blue jackets, faced with white or red, and were armed with re-volvers and swords. The Colonial Volunteers, grouped in corps of various names, wore an assortment of uniform after the style of Colonel Durnford, commander of the Reserve Column, who described his costume in a letter to his mother as "boots, spurs, dark cord breeches, serge patrol jacket, broad belt over the shoulders and another round the waist, revolver, hunting knife, ammunition pouch, wide-awake felt hat, turned up on one side with a crimson ribbon." "Very like a stage brigand," he observed. The troopers carried a Swinburn–Martini carbine, to which an American "Bowie" knife had been adapted to fit as a bayonet.

A soldier of soldiers, Anthony Durnford was described by his contemporaries as a man with all his heart in his profession, keen, active, indefatigable, unsparing of himself, utterly fear-less, honourable, loyal, of great kindness and goodness of heart, loved and respected by his men. Born in Ireland in 1830 and commissioned a second lieutenant with the Royal Engineers

[30]

in 1848, Durnford in 1872 came to South Africa, where he served in the suppression of several native uprisings. In one of these he was severely wounded, losing the use of his left arm.

First-rate soldier he may have been, but was he prone to rashness, to acting too often on his own authority? There are definite indications that he was impetuous, apt to take his own line and act on his own initiative: that he believed he knew better than his commander. He was ever eager to get to grips with the enemy, hating, in his own words, "to be left behind." He knew more of native warfare than any other officer; he understood and liked the natives, and he was trusted by them. He thought highly of Cetewayo, to whose coronation he had accompanied Shepstone. He believed, with his friend Bishop Colenso, that the Zulu king was anxious for a peaceful settlement and did not want war—controversial views that made Durnford unpopular with the colonists and the authorities, but that showed him to have the sort of independent mind that is seldom an advantage to a military career.

Durnford's Commander in Chief, Lord Chelmsford, was a man of very different mould, one of those delightful donkeys by whom the British army was afflicted for a hundred years. Amiable, affable, charming, gracious, a gentleman from his flowing whiskers to his aristocratic fingertips, Chelmsford suffered from just those weaknesses that appear to have been the requisite for British high command in the nineteenth century and after. He changed his mind quickly and often; he fussed over minor things and missed essentials; he was weak and uncertain, punctilious without exactness. He ambled when he should have hurried, and hurried when he should have hesitated.

Chelmsford, born Frederick Augustus Thesiger, the son of a Lord Chancellor, joined the Grenadier Guards in 1844, becoming a captain by 1850, a major in 1855, a colonel in 1863, and a brigadier general in 1877, being raised to the local rank of lieutenant general on his appointment to command the British forces in South Africa. He had served in the Crimean War and on the staff of Sir Robert Napier in the Abyssinian campaign in 1868, being praised after the capture of Magdala for "great ability and untiring energy," which proves only that he was a conscientious underling.

He had all the right ideas: "In conducting operations against an enemy like the Zulu, the first blow struck should be a heavy one, and I am satisfied that no greater mistake can be made than to attempt to conquer him with insufficient means. He has the advantage of being able to march in one day at least three times as far as the British soldier, and he has no commissariat train to hamper him." He told Sir Bartle Frere, "If we are to have a fight with the Zulus, I am anxious that our arrangements should be as complete as it is possible to make them. Half measures do not answer with natives. They must be thoroughly crushed to make them believe in our superiority; and if I am called upon to conduct operations against them, I shall strive to be in a position to show them how hopelessly inferior they are to us in fighting power although numerically stronger."

Lord Chelmsford took his responsibilities most seriously. He made a close study of all that was known of the organisation of the Zulu army and its tactics, the management of native troops, the care of horses and mules, the difficulties of transport and commissariat. He drew up rules for installing regimental depots, building field hospitals, taking sanitary precautions, and for entrenching and laagering the camp at night. These rules he had printed in a pamphlet entitled *Regulations for Field Forces in South Africa*, which he distributed to his

officers, many of whom considered it a reflection on their
military ability that they could hardly welcome. Lord Chelmsford even took the trouble to discuss Zulu tactics with Paul
Kruger, the Boer leader and future President, who warned him
of the Zulus' amazing mobility, capacity for concealment, and
ability to stage large movements with perfect timing. Kruger
urged upon him the vital need for laagering his camp at night,
every night, and the necessity for always scouting a considerable distance ahead—advice to which Lord Chelmsford listened
politely but later neglected to put to use.

The reports Lord Chelmsford received of the Zulu army
were highly conflicting. No one denied that its warriors were
brave, highly disciplined, savage beyond description, and could
become mad with battle lust. Some informants said they would
fight to the last ditch; others said the army would revolt
against Cetewayo, or fail to stand up to the fire of cannon and
the British soldiers' volleys. The Zulus were well supplied with
guns, both ancient muskets and modern breechloaders, many
of which were surplus British army material sold to specu-
lators by the War Office at two guns for one shilling, and
passed on by gunrunners at the price of a gun for five head of
cattle, a charge that competition forced down to a gun for
two head of cattle. But the Zulus' traditional and chief weapon
was the assegai, the short stabbing spear that had been designed
by Shaka. Another, a throwing assegai, was held in the left
hand along with a great oxhide shield, protecting the warrior
from throat to ankle. The muskets and rifles were carried
chiefly by the older men, who could afford to buy them; but
they played little part in the campaign, for the Zulu fire was
almost invariably wild.

There follows an excerpt from the lengthy portion of

Lord Chelmsford's pamphlet that was devoted to a study of the Zulu army, its organisation and tactics.

The Zulu army, which may be estimated at from 40,000 to 50,000 men [which events proved to be a considerable overestimate, for not more than 25,000 Zulus took the field at any one time], is composed of the entire nation capable of bearing arms. The method employed in recruiting its ranks is as follows: At short intervals, varying from two to five years, all the young men who have during that time attained the age of 14 or 15 years are formed into a regiment, which, after a year's probation, during which they are supposed to pass from boyhood and its duties to manhood, is placed at a military kraal or headquarters. In some cases they are sent to an already existing kraal, which is the headquarters of a corps or regiment, of which they then become part; in others, especially when the young regiment is numerous, they build a new military kraal. As the regiment grows old it generally has one or more regiments embodied with it, so that the young men may have the benefit of their elders' experience, and when the latter gradually die out, may take their place and keep up the name and prestige of their military kraal. In this manner corps are formed, often many thousands strong, such, for instance, as the Undi.

Under this system, then, the Zulu army has gradually increased until at present it consists of 12 corps, and two regiments, each possessing its own military kraal. The corps necessarily contains men of all ages, some being married and wearing the head-ring, others unmarried; some being old men scarcely able to walk, while others are hardly out of their teens. Indeed five of these corps are now composed of a single regiment each, which has absorbed the original but practically non-existent regiment to which it had been affiliated.

Each of these corps or regiments has the same internal formation. They are in the first place divided equally into two wings—the right and the left—and in the second are subdivided into companies from 10 to 200 in number, according to the numerical strength of the corps or regiment to which they belong, and which is estimated at 50 men each, with the exception of the Nkobamakesi Regiment, which averages 70 to the company.

Each corps or regiment, possessing its own military kraal, has the following officers:—One commanding officer (called the chief induna), one second-in-command (called the second induna), who directly commands the left wing, and two wing officers. Besides the above there are company officers, consisting of a captain and from one to three junior officers, all of whom are of the same age as the men they command, while in the case of a corps the commanding officer of each regiment composing it takes rank next to its four great officers when he is himself not one of them.

The chief distinction is between married and unmarried men. No one in Zululand, male or female, is permitted to marry without the direct permission of the King, and when he allows a regiment to do so, which is not before the men are about 40 years of age, they have to shave the crown of the head, and to put a ring round it, and then they become one of the "white" regiments, carrying white shields etc. in contradistinction to the "black" or unmarried regiments, who wear their hair naturally and have coloured shields.

The total number of regiments in the Zulu army is 33, of whom 18 are formed of men with rings on their heads, and 15 of unmarried men. Seven of the former are composed of men over 60 years of age, so that for practical purposes there are not more than 26 Zulu regiments able to take the field, numbering altogether 40,000. Of these 22,500 are betwen 20 and 30 years of age, 10,000 between 30 and 40, 3,400 between 40 and 50, and 4,500 between 50 and 60 years of age. From which it will be seen the mortality in Zululand is unusually rapid.

Drill—in the ordinary acceptance of the term—is un-

known among Zulus; the few simple movements which
they perform with any method, such as forming a circle
of companies or regiments, breaking into companies or
regiments from the circle, forming a line of march in
order of companies, or in close order of regiments, not
being deserving of the name. The officers have, however,
their regulated duties and responsibilities, according to
their rank, and the men lend a ready obedience to their
orders.

As might be expected, a savage army like that of
Zululand neither has nor requires much commissariat or
transport. The former consists of three or four days'
provisions in the shape of maize or millet, and a herd of
cattle, proportioned to the distance to be traversed, ac-
companies each regiment. The latter consists of a number
of lads who follow each regiment, carrying the sleeping
mats, blankets, and provisions, and assisting to drive the
cattle.

When a Zulu army on the line of march come to a
river in flood, and the breadth of the stream which is out
of their depth does not exceed from 10 to 15 yards, they
plunge in in a dense mass, holding on to one another,
those behind forcing them forward, and thus succeed in
crossing with the loss of a few of their number.

In the event of hostilities arising between the Zulu
nation and any other (unless some very sudden attack was
made on their country), messengers would be sent,
travelling night and day if necessary, by the King to
order the men to assemble in regiments at their respective
military kraals, where they would find the commanding
officer ready to receive them. When a corps or regiment
has thus congregated at its headquarters, it would, on
receiving the order, proceed to the King's kraal. Before
marching, a circle is formed inside the kraal, each company together, their officers in an inner ring—the first
and second in command in the centre. The regiment then
proceeds to break into companies, beginning from the
left-hand side, each company forming a circle, and

marching off followed by boys carrying provisions, mats, etc. The company officers march immediately in rear of their men, the second-in-command in rear of the left wing, and the commanding officer in rear of the right.

On arriving at the King's kraal each regiment encamps on its own ground, as no two regiments can be trusted not to fight if encamped together. The following ceremonies are then performed:

All the regiments being formed into an immense circle a little distance from the King's kraal, the officers form an inner ring surrounding the chief officers and the King, together with the doctors and medicine basket.

A doctored beast is then killed, it is cut into strips, powdered with medicine, and taken round to the men by the chief medicine men, the soldiers not touching it with their hands, but biting a piece of the strip held out to them. They are then dismissed for the day with orders to assemble in the morning. The next day early they all take emetics, form a circle, and are again dismissed. On the third day they again form a circle of regiments, are then sprinkled with medicine by the doctors and receive their orders through the chief officer of state present, perhaps receiving an address from the King, after which they start on their expedition.

Previous to marching off the regiments reform companies under their respective officers, and the regiment selected by the King to take the lead advances. The march is in order of companies for the first day, after which it is continued in the path, which may be explained by likening it to one of our divisions advancing in line of brigade columns, each brigade in mass; each regiment in close column; the line of provision bearers, etc. move on the flank; the intervals between heads of columns varying according to circumstances, from several miles to within sight of each other; constant communication is kept up by runners.

The march would be continued in this order, with the exception that the baggage and provision bearers fall in rear of the column on the second day, and that the cattle composing the commissariat are driven between them and the rearmost regiment until near the enemy. The order of companies is then resumed, and on coming in sight, the whole army again forms a circle, for the purpose of enabling the Commander-in-Chief to address the men, and give his final instructions, which concluded, the different regiments intended to commence the attack do so.

A large body of troops, as a reserve, remain seated with their backs to the enemy; the commanders and staff retire to some eminence with one or two of the older regiments (as extra reserves).

All orders are delivered by runners.

It is to be noted that although the above were the ordinary customs of the Zulu army when at war, it is more than probable that great changes, both in movement and dress, will be made consequent on the introduction of firearms among them.

Zulu attack formations were shown by a diagram, and notes were supplied giving the title of each regiment, and the name of its commanding officer, with details of its distinguishing dress and shield markings. The most important information related to the deployment of the impis in attack: "It consists of what the Zulus term the horns, the chest, and the body of the army, corresponding with our wings, support and reserve. It is the duty of the horns, which really take the shape of horns converging inwards, to circle round the flanks of the enemy, only a few men forming the points of the horn, which gradually increase to ten, twelve, or more at the base. The enemy once encompassed by the horns, the chest advances in open, but deep order; then follows the main body in a dense mass, with crushing effect."

This Zulu formation, as old in military history as the battle of Cannae (216 B.C.), was the invention of Shaka, who created an army that marked a radical departure in primitive warfare, a striking force that could have given the Romans a beating. At the start of the campaign the Zulu army, and particularly its encircling tactics, were held cheap by the British, prone, as usual, to underrate enemies with black skins. A member of the Natal Legislature confidently advised Frere that "with a hundred redcoats you might march from one end of Zululand to the other."

Lord Chelmsford planned to invade Zululand in four columns, crossing the 200-mile frontier at different points and converging on Ulundi, situated fifty-five miles due east of the Natal frontier at Rorke's Drift. He abandoned the idea of a single mass drive on Cetewayo's capital for fear that the Zulu impis might creep round him, cut his communications, invade Natal and massacre the colonists. It would be easier, too, considered Lord Chelmsford, for separate columns to advance and bring up supplies over the trackless wastes of Zululand. The four columns would push the Zulus before them like a flock of frightened sheep, until the impis were conveniently collected at Ulundi, where he would crush them with one great blow, that is if they fought at all. He rejected the suggestion that the combined Zulu impis might try to destroy his columns piecemeal. To Frere he wrote:

> The plan I have laid down as necessary is not so ambitious a one as a rapid march upon Ulundi and the occupation of the king's kraal, but I am certain it is the only safe one under the circumstances. It would be impossible to keep a long line of road passable for a convoy of wagons, and were we to advance far into the country it would be almost certain that, instead of our supplies coming to us, we should have to return for them. A retrograde movement would have a very bad effect on our native forces and would encourage our enemies.

The Zulu frontier Lord Chelmsford now faced was separated from Natal on the north by the Blood River, which, merging into the Tugela just above Rorke's Drift, delineated the frontier as far as the sea. He drew up his columns at three river crossings, the left column, commanded by Col. Henry Evelyn Wood, V.C. at Utrecht, on the northern frontier of Zululand; the central column (with which Chelmsford proposed to go himself), under Colonel Glyn, at Rorke's Drift; the right column, commanded by Colonel Pearson, at the mouth of the Tugela. Ulundi lay at the apex of the triangle.

On the expected failure of Cetewayo to satisfy the terms of the ultimatum, all three columns were to cross the river, leaving Colonel Durnford with his native contingent, 3,871 strong, in the rear of the middle column, ready to support it or to move into Zululand independently as circumstances dictated. The British soldiers and twenty fieldpieces were distributed evenly amongst the three advance columns, and they and Durnford's column were equipped also with rocket batteries, tubes and troughs, carried on muleback, which, when set up on the ground, could fire, up to a distance of 1,200 yards, rockets carrying an explosive charge of between three and twelve pounds. Their effect was small, for the wily Zulus quickly learned to scatter when they saw a rocket coming. (These "Hale" rockets in 1860 had replaced the Congreve rocket, which had been employed in European warfare since 1814. Their use was discontinued in 1885.)

Colonel Glyn had 4,659 officers and men at his command. These included 20 staff officers; 132 artillerymen; 1,275 British infantry—the 1st and 2nd Battalions of the 24th Foot; 320 Colonial Horse; 2,566 native levies; and 346 wagonmen. The artillery carried six 7-pound guns and two rocket troughs. In the wagon train were 1,507 oxen, 49 horses and 67 mules, accompanied by 220 wagons and 82 carts.

On January 4, the day of the official notification to Cetewayo, Lord Chelmsford moved his headquarters to Helpmakaar, close to Rorke's Drift, from where he wrote to his friend Frere that "our cause is a good one," expressing the hope that before many weeks had passed he would be able to convince the Zulus that "for a savage, as for a child, timely severity is greater kindness than mistaken leniency."

In Natal and Zululand it was high summer, wet, humid, hot, in contrast to the severe winter then being experienced in both Britain and in the United States, where, for the first time in living memory, there was ice in Florida. In England the people took only a languid interest in the prospects of war in Zululand, to the location of which they were completely hazy. There was fearful distress and poverty in the industrial north, thousands of poor people being kept alive by municipal soup kitchens. In London hundreds died every week in an epidemic of smallpox. All over Britain indignant members of the Aborigines Protection Society were signing their names to a petition to the government protesting Britain's wanton aggression against King Cetewayo.

Cetewayo mobilised his army. From all over Zululand the regiments converged on Ulundi. He was determined not to make the first move. If the British crossed the frontier, drive them out, he told his generals. Under no circumstances were the impis to cross the frontier, he ordered. Assaults on fortified positions were forbidden. Cetewayo did not go to war himself. Fat and indolent, he waited in his kraal. The war was not of his making, and he knew that in a pitched battle his savage warriors would be no match for the British. He hoped that his impis would catch them unawares and destroy them piecemeal. Cetewayo was no great general like his ancestor Shaka. Bewildered by the British aggression, he awaited a saving miracle.

In Pietermaritzburg Sir Bartle Frere predicted a speedy settlement of the Zulu problem. He could confidently look forward to a peerage as his just reward. He may have looked even higher; a coronet dangled before his eyes.

5

THE INVASION
OF ZULULAND

Lord chelmsford sat on his horse, gazing across the Buffalo River at the mountains and hills of Zululand stretching away in the distance. Below him he could see the mission house at Rorke's Drift at the foot of a steep and precipitous cliff, beyond it the river crossing, his jumping-off place for the invasion of Cetewayo's country scheduled to start at dawn next morning, January 11. The night before he had written to his Commander in Chief in London, the Duke of Cambridge, telling his Royal Highness:

> It is impossible to speculate what tactics the Zulus will pursue. Reports say that the country is in a state of utter confusion, and I have no doubt that orders and counterorders from Cetewayo will still further perplex those upon whom he depends for the protection of his country. Our movements will all be made in the most deliberate manner. There is nothing to be gained by a rapid forward movement, and if I wished to make a rush, I should be unable to carry it out, consequent upon the great dif-

ficulties of supply and transport. . . . We are now also in the most rainy season of the year, and convoys are sadly delayed by the state of the roads. I may possibly therefore be unable to finish the war with that rapidity which, under the present aspect of affairs in Europe, is evidently so desirable. Your Royal Highness however, may rest assured that I shall do my best to bring it to a speedy close, so that I may be enabled to send back to England some of the regiments now under my command.

The bugles sounded reveille at daybreak on January 11. Private Henry Hook, of the 24th Regiment, whose company had been ordered to guard the supply depot and hospital at Rorke's Drift, came down to the Buffalo River to watch the river crossing and say good-bye to his friends. The thick mist turned to a damp, depressing drizzle as the column began its invasion of Zululand. By 6:30 A.M. the infantry were across and spreading out in skirmishing order. A camp was formed on the Zulu bank, and during the day the wagons and guns were ferried across. There was no opposition. That morning the *Times* of Natal printed a "notification" from Sir Bartle Frere:

> The British Forces are crossing into Zululand to exact from Cetewayo reparations for violations of British Territory committed by the sons of Sirayo and others, and to enforce compliance with the promises made by Cetewayo at his Coronation for the better government of his people.
>
> The British Government has no quarrel with the Zulu people. All Zulus who come in unarmed, or who lay down their arms, will be provided for till the troubles of their country are over, and will then, if they please, be allowed to return to their own land; but all who do not so submit will be dealt with as enemies.
>
> When the war is finished, the British Government will

make the best arrangements in its power for the future
good government of the Zulus in their own country, in
peace and quietness, and will not permit the killing and
oppression they have suffered from Cetewayo to continue.

In his final instructions, Frere had told Lord Chelmsford:

You will virtually annex and settle the country, as you
proceed, and greatly simplify proceedings when Cetewayo is disposed of. I have no idea of recommending any
revival of a paramount chief or king or of any separate
Zulu nationality. An active and absolute Military Admin-
istrator, with a firm grasp of the country, by means of the
pick of your native Regiments as Sepoys and Police, and
supported by a backbone of H.M. Troops, will keep
order among the chiefs who submit and obey, and will
after putting down opposition govern directly, through
headmen . . . all as subjects of Queen Victoria. I am not
reckoning my chickens before they are hatched, but
merely sketching what should I think be our object in the,
I trust now inevitable, event of the Zulu being relieved
from the monster who has so long been an incubus to
them as well as a terror to his neighbours.

On January 12, Lord Chelmsford's troops had their first
brush with the Zulus. Moving off at 3:30 A.M., four companies
of the 1st Battalion 24th Regiment, supported by a contingent
of native levies, advanced on Sirayo's kraal nine miles away. As
they approached within 500 yards a voice was heard crying:
"By whose orders has the white impi come here. Are you
enemies?" When no answer was given, a heavy fire came from
amongst the krantzes—steep walls of rock—above the kraal.
The Zulus were speedily dislodged, thirty being killed, the
British losing two natives. The whole action was over by
9 A.M., and the kraal's stock, consisting of five hundred cattle,

was rounded up. The kraal was ordered to be burnt. Lord Chelmsford wrote that evening to tell Frere of his first success:

I am in great hopes that the news of the storming of Sirayo's stronghold and the capture of so many of his cattle may have a salutary effect in Zululand and either bring down a large force to attack us or else produce a revolution in the country. Sirayo's men have, I am told, always been looked upon as the bravest in the country, and certainly those who were killed today fought with great courage. I have visited two wounded Zulus who are in our hospital and have seen that they are well looked after. Directly they are well enough I shall let them go, so that they may tell their friends how the British make war. The country is in a terrible state from the rain, and I do not know how we shall manage to get our wagons across the valley near Sirayo's kraal.

Norris Newman, the war correspondent of the London *Standard*, took the opportunity of the raid on the kraal to ride to the top of the hill above it, writing home next day:

The sight obtained was magnificent. Looking down a precipitous cliff, a splendid valley extended for miles, rich in verdure, covered with deserted kraals, and bounded on each side by high mountains, while to the south the Buffalo river and the Natal mountains were seen in the distance, with our camp at Rorke's Drift, looking like a miniature tin soldiers' camp. To the east-ward, the Isipezi Hill rose in the air with its curious shaped head, and close by it was our road to Ulundi. Al-together it was a sight worth seeing.

Between the eminence on which he stood and Isipezi Hill in the distance Newman noticed a grotesque outcrop of rock, small in comparison with the hills close to it, but standing well out from its surroundings; this was Isandhlwana Mount,

Isandhlwana meaning "Little Hand" in Zulu. He thought it looked like a crouching lion or a stone sphinx. ("Little Sphinx" the men of the 24th Regiment came to call it, for its shape bore a remarkable resemblance to the figure on their regimental badge.) He would be able to inspect it more closely within a few days, he was told, for the road to Ulundi passed between the Mount and a little hill to its right.

For seven days the column made no further advance. The road needed to be drained and rebuilt, and supplies brought across the Buffalo. Every day terrific thunderstorms would rage over the hills, the heavy rain making the road more and more impassable. Bad places were filled with rocks so that the wagons could pass.

On January 14 Lord Chelmsford received a communication that vexed him greatly. A report came from Colonel Durnford, waiting at Kranzkop to join the advance into Zululand, who stated he had been told by a missionary that a Zulu impi was gathering to cross the Buffalo just above Rorke's Drift. He said he was moving off in force to prevent the invasion of Natal. Chelmsford ordered him to return to base at once, giving him a good ticking off:

> Unless you carry out the instructions I give you, it will be my unpleasant duty to remove you from your command, and to substitute another officer for the command of No. 2 Column. When a column is acting SEPARATELY in an *enemy's country* I am quite ready to give its commander every latitude, and would certainly expect him to disobey any orders he might receive from me, if information which he obtained showed that it would be injurious to the interests of the column under his command. Your neglecting to obey my instructions in the present instance has no excuse. You have simply received information in a letter from Bishop Schroeder,

which may or may not be true and which you have no means of verifying. If movements ordered are to be delayed because report hints at a chance of an invasion of Natal, it will be impossible for me to carry out my plan of campaign. I trust you will understand this plain speaking and not give me any further occasion to write in a style which is distasteful to me.

When this letter was brought to Durnford, "a look of disgust crossed his face," according to a brother officer. A few days later Durnford's unauthorised move was cited as an example of his insubordination and inclination to rashness.

During the delay in the advance Lord Chelmsford was visited by a Boer leader, J. J. Uys, a man experienced in Zulu fighting, who warned him, "Be on your guard and be careful. Trek into Zululand with two laagers close to each other. Place your spies far out and form your wagons into a round laager at night. The Zulus are more dangerous than you think. I have lost my father and brother through them, because we held them too cheaply."* Sage advice, which Lord Chelmsford ignored. At Uys's words, he smiled and said he thought laagering was not necessary—an example of Lord Chelmsford's overconfidence, which Durnford's supporters cited as the true cause of the disaster that overtook his army.

While his soldiers struggled to make the road passable, Lord Chelmsford and his staff rode ahead to select a site for the next camp, picking upon the narrow plateau immediately to the east of Isandhlwana Mount, a flat-topped, elongated hill with precipitous sides, situated ten miles from Rorke's Drift, approximately the distance Lord Chelmsford considered practical for the next advance. This was a choice that Norris Newman

* At Italeni, 1838.

described a few days later as "an error of judgement," to which he could not help attributing "the awful result."

The Mount, a boulder-strewn crag approximately 300 yards long at the summit and accessible only from the north, rises from north to south, and is connected by a narrow ridge or "neck," over which runs the road, to a koppie named Stoney Hill, immediately to the south. The ground to the north and south of the Mount is rugged and broken. From its eastern escarpment a plateau slopes gently down for half a mile to a dry water-course, running parallel to the length of the hill, and opening on to a plain that is four miles wide and extends for eight miles, and that is bounded on the north and south by hills. While the view to the front is extensive, the hills on the north and south, the Ngutu and Ndhlazagazi ranges, obscure the view on either flank.

Satisfied with his choice, Lord Chelmsford ordered the camp to be moved up next day and pitched on the plateau facing the plain, with Isandhlwana Mount protecting its rear. Critics of the choice have suggested that it was a dangerous one for an army expecting attack, for the rough ground to the north and south was unlikely to afford any protection against nimble-footed Zulus, accustomed from childhood to bounding from crag to crag and charging over broken, rocky ground. Critics have claimed further that the encircling hills provided perfect concealment for thousands of warriors, which in fact they did. But Lord Chelmsford was limited as to the distance the camp could be moved, and he did not expect to be attacked. He thought the Zulus would retreat before him.

By midday on January 20, most of the troops had been moved up to Isandhlwana: but at nightfall many of the wagons were still on their way from Rorke's Drift. Despite the stringent regulations he himself had laid down, Lord Chelmsford made no attempt to entrench or laager the camp, either that night or the next. The regulations for encampment had stated:

> The camp should be formed in such a manner that the troops can be rapidly placed in a good position for action in the event of a night attack. By night the horses should be piquetted, and oxen placed in wagon laager, the camp guarded by outlying piquets of infantry thrown out at short distances to the front, flanks and rear, with small parties of natives, ten men in each, interspersed and placed in situations where they could give timely warning of the approach of the enemy. The camp should be partially entrenched on all sides.

Several officers privately voiced their misgivings about the choice of the site, the failure to laager the camp and the inadequacy of the patrols sent out to guard it against surprise.

Lt. Teignmouth Melville of the 24th Regiment, of whose great deeds we shall hear later, came upon a staff officer looking out at the front of the camp. The expression on his face led Melville to say, "I know what you are thinking, sir; you are abusing this camp and you are quite right. These Zulus will charge home, and with our small numbers we ought to be in laager, or, at any rate, prepared to stand shoulder to shoulder." The officer replied that he did not like the situation and had spoken of it favourably only from a sense of his official position. As the two officers walked back to the tents, he told Melville he had a strong presentiment of evil. The staff officer was not in the camp when the disaster he foresaw struck. Melville died in sight of safety.

Subinspector F. L. Phillips of the Natal Mounted Police was even more emphatic. Knowing the Zulus and their tactics well, he buttonholed Colonel Crealock, Lord Chelmsford's Military Secretary. The Zulus, he pointed out, could be lurking in the hills on the left and right flank and could approach to within striking distance of the camp without being seen. They could run as fast as cavalry. He urged the need to laager the camp. Crealock brought him a reply from Lord Chelmsford: "Tell the police officer my troops will do all the attacking. If the enemy does venture to attack, the hills he complains of will protect our rear."

The story told by Police Captain Mansell is even more extraordinary. Ordered to take a patrol towards the Ngutu Hills, he was told not to go too far. When he suggested that he reconnoitre the crest of the hills he was informed that that would be of no use. To his complaint that the country north of the camp was very broken and could easily conceal a whole impi, a staff officer told him, "My dear fellow, mounted vedettes are useless there; the rear always protects itself." Mansell felt he was going on a fool's errand, an impression that was strengthened when he captured an aged Zulu who told him: "Why are you looking for the Zulus this way? The big impi is coming from that direction," and pointed to the crest of the Ngutu Hills. When Mansell gave this information to Lord Chelmsford at dinner that night, the General said it was of no importance.

While the tents were being pitched, Lord Chelmsford and his staff, with an escort of Colonial Volunteers, rode in a south-easterly direction for about nine miles to reconnoitre a rocky fastness known to be the chief Matyana's stronghold, and believed to be then occupied by that chief and his retainers. It consisted of a deep ravine or glen with precipitous sides, through which ran the Amangene stream that formed a waterfall at its head and eventually joined the Buffalo River. From the high ground overlooking this chasm no signs of a Zulu force could be perceived, and the General returned to

[5 1]

the camp, arriving there about 6:30 P.M., by which time the troops under Colonel Glyn had settled down.

The line was composed of one company each of British and native troops. The 24th Regiment was on piquet on the right and the native contingent on the left. By night this outpost line was brought to within about 500 yards of the tents, and was made continuous, encircling the camp and Isandhlwana Mount. Meanwhile a detached piquet of the native contingent was stationed some 1,200 yards to the north.

Lord Chelmsford's headquarters, together with the hospital tents, was positioned in the immediate rear; behind them stood 150 wagons, the rest having become stuck in a water course a mile west of the camp, where they were guarded all night by a company of redcoats.

Early next morning, January 21, in furtherance of his plan to clear the country of the enemy, Chelmsford sent out a force of 150 mounted police and sixteen companies of the native contingent, under Major Dartnell, to examine the high ground southeast of the camp that he had himself reconnoitred the afternoon before. With Dartnell went Captain Lonsdale and Commander W. Drummond in charge of the natives. Two of Lord Chelmsford's A.D.C.'s, Major Gossett and Capt. E. H. Buller, accompanied the party. On reaching Matyana's stronghold, Lonsdale led his men up the steep sides of the glen, densely covered with thorny bush, to the top of the Ndhlazagazi range of hills. There was no sign of the enemy, and they captured some cattle. "Presently," tells trooper Symons, "We heard the report of a gun away to the left. Not another sound was heard, not even a bird broke the stillness with its note." The shot had come from one of Major Dartnell's men; ascending the hill to the left of the glen they came suddenly upon about 700 Zulus, their white shields glistening in the sun, trotting in a northerly direction. When a small party under Captain Mansell was sent to make a show of force, the Zulus turned towards them, advancing and throwing out their horns. As it was now getting late in the afternoon, Major Dartnell decided to withdraw towards the camp, sending a message back by Major Gossett asking for food and blankets, as he wished to bivouac for the night. Dartnell's news confirmed a report Lord Chelmsford had received at 4:30 P.M. from Gamdana, a brother of Sirayo's who had surrendered, that he had heard the Umcityu Regiment was assembled not far from Isipezi Hill.

Trooper Symons takes up the story of Dartnell's force:

Marching back to a clear little stream, we halted and off-saddled. The police had brought camp kettles on their pack horses, but we had nothing to make tea in. However, the police got little satisfaction from their cooking-pots; for just as the water was on the point of boiling, the order came to saddle-up. Tired and disappointed, we stood to our horses and mounting, followed the major over the hill in the enemy's direction. Six Carabineers were sent on to reconnoitre. We anxiously watched them, as they disappeared over the brow, but had not long to wait before they came back at a gallop, down the stony mountain side. Then appeared, as if by magic, from one end of the ridge to the other, a long line of black men in skirmishing order, advancing at a run. It was a grand sight and they never uttered a sound. I defy the men of any British regiment to keep their intervals so well at the double. On reaching the brow of the hill, the centre halted and then the horns appeared. The points of the horns were half-way down, and all thought we were to be attacked. Nevertheless, we held our positions when the Zulus, of whom there were some seven or eight

[53]

hundred, turned (for what reason I cannot say, unless it was to entice us up the mountain into a trap) and slowly retired, leaving only three or four men visible.

Thinking that he was in touch with the fringe of a great impi, Major Dartnell sent a further message to the camp stating that he did not consider the force at his disposal sufficient to attack the Zulus and requesting that a reinforcement of two or three companies of the 24th be sent out so he could attack the enemy in the morning.

Trooper Symons provides us with the story of the night in Dartnell's bivouac:

By this time, we were all pretty well famished, and there was a little grumbling on hearing that we were to bivouac that night without food or blankets. As we retraced our steps, the native force met us and we marched together to a favourable spot on an open piece of ground close to a stream. It was a great relief to be rid of our heavy rifles and cartridges, which had not been off our shoulders since 4 A.M. On the opposite side of the spruit stood some kraals and here some of us collected some spinach, which we cooked to make a frugal meal.

That night nine men were told off for camp guard, the remainder taking it in turns, three at a time to hold the horses, which had been linked together within the camp. A hollow square had been formed. Macfarlane, Stirton and I were on first relief guard, and during our watch some mounted infantry arrived from the camp with provisions and blankets. The food soon vanished and the blankets were distributed among the men. Someone else got the benefit of mine.

The guards' orders were to hold the horses in the event of an alarm. When the second relief took over, the natives had lighted great fires and were talking in loud voices, but the hum gradually subsided. The horses stood perfectly still, for they were too tired to move. We three of the first relief were sharing blankets, and I was almost asleep when a shot was fired away in front. I was on the alert, you may be sure, in two winks. "Mac," I called, "did you hear that?" "Yes," said he, jumping up.

I seized my rifle and ran to my post, which was no sooner reached than with one accord those 2,000 natives rose, striking their shields, firing off their guns and losing all control over themselves. Some ran among the horses and had to be beaten back with clubbed rifles. Many found their way back to Natal that night; others were wounded by the assegais of their comrades who mistook them for Zulus. I could hear Captain Shepstone's voice giving the order to fall in, but I could see nothing. Now and then, the sergeant-major of the police roared out in stentorian tones, "Halt. Who goes there?" He never got an answer, but he told his men not to fire. The horses were stampeding and, when the din had ceased, it was some time before they could be collected.

Back at Isandhlwana, after the party carrying food and blankets to Major Dartnell had left, the piquets and mounted vedettes were withdrawn towards the camp perimeter, and the camp settled down for the night. War correspondent Norris Newman recalls the last night the British troops spent at Isandhlwana:

Our mess had a jolly little dinner at which a few guests were present and afterwards many other comrades looked in for a chat. Poor Charlie Pope; that was the last occasion on which I saw him alive, and many others recall even now how sorry he was at not being able to join our party in the morning, and how eagerly he looked forward (like others) to the first real fight with the enemy.

Five miles to the northeast of the camp a Zulu impi, 20,000 strong, lay hidden in the rocky krantzes of the Ngutu Hills.

They lit no fires; they made no sound. From their points of observation, their chiefs watched the distant campfires grow dim. An occasional flicker threw up the shapes of the sentries as they paced up and down calling "All's well" to their comrades.

6

DECOY

D ARTNELL'S DECISION to bivouac where he stood did not please Lord Chelmsford, and the latter was even more vexed when he was roused at 1:30 A.M. to receive a further report from the Major that the enemy was in greater strength than he had anticipated, and that he needed reinforcements.

It sounded very much as if Dartnell was in touch with the fringe of the Zulu impi that rumour said had left Ulundi some days before. Accepting the situation and determined to seek out the Zulus, Chelmsford ordered Colonel Glyn to move to Dartnell's support at daybreak, taking with him six companies of the 2nd Battalion 24th Regiment, four of the heavy guns, and the Mounted Infantry and the Native Pioneer Corps. These troops, added to Dartnell's force, would represent half the centre column's strength. He would accompany the troops himself, Chelmsford said, for whether or not they brought the Zulus to battle, he proposed to push on past Isipezi Hill to select a site for the next camp. Lord Chelmsford issued two further orders that were to lead to heated controversy and violent dispute after the disaster.

Col. Henry Pulleine, commanding the 1st Battalion 24th

Regiment, was instructed to defend the camp in Colonel Glyn's
absence, and to be ready to strike the tents and camp equipage
belonging to the advance force and to send it on if requested.
What exactly Pulleine was ordered to do to protect the camp
was described by Major Clery, Glyn's staff officer. Clery,
speaking from memory after the disaster, said he had told
Pulleine, "You will be in command of the camp in the absence
of Colonel Glyn; draw in your camp or your line of defence
[he couldn't remember which he said] while the force is out;
also draw in the line of your infantry outposts accordingly,
but keep your cavalry vedettes still far advanced." A wagon
loaded with ammunition was to be kept ready to follow the
force marching out, in case they should be seriously engaged.
Major Clery stated he believed he told Pulleine that Colonel
Durnford had been ordered to bring up his troops to strengthen
the camp.

But a captain of the 24th Regiment who went out with
Lord Chelmsford and survived the day, some years later told
Colonel Durnford's brother (he was collecting information to
absolve the Colonel from blame for what happened at Isandhlwana) that no explicit orders were given to Colonel Pulleine,
and that he had heard Lord Chelmsford ask when they were
some miles from the camp, "What orders have been left for
Colonel Pulleine?"

The second order was sent to Colonel Durnford, who had
been left, much to his chagrin, at Rorke's Drift with his Natal
Native Contingent. The exact wording of this order was
questioned after the battle. The actual order was never found;
but at the court of enquiry set up by Lord Chelmsford to
collect evidence after the disaster, Colonel Crealock stated
that the order had read, "Move up to Isandhlwana camp at
once with all your mounted men and rocket battery; take

command of it. I am accompanying Colonel Glyn, who is moving off at once to attack Matyana and a Zulu force said to be twelve or fourteen miles off, and at present watched by Natal Police, the Volunteers, and the Natal Native Contingent. Colonel Glyn takes with him the 2nd Battalion of the 24th Regiment, four guns, and the Mounted Infantry." The words "take command" formed the basis of blame attributed to Colonel Durnford.

But, apparently, the order to Colonel Durnford did not contain these vital words. When the ghastly field of Isandhl-wana was revisited by British troops some months later, Colonel Crealock's mud-stained notebook was found near his tent. The orders to Durnford he had taken down at Lord Chelmsford's dictation stated only, "You are to march to this camp *at once* with all the force you have with you." There was no order to take command. That does not, however, en-tirely settle the vexing question of who was in actual command of the camp at Isandhlwana on January 22 and thus responsible for the disaster; for Colonel Durnford on reaching the camp would, as Colonel Pulleine's senior officer, automatically have assumed command. But, as will be seen, Colonel Durnford, on reaching the camp, immediately left it.

Lord Chelmsford's somewhat ambiguous order to Durnford was carried by a young lieutenant employed on transport duties, Horace Smith-Dorrien, who had been sent out from England at Chelmsford's special request, a young man destined to survive the awful day and to become famous in British military history as a general in World War I.

Smith-Dorrien set out to ride the ten miles to Rorke's Drift just as dawn was breaking. Looking back in his old age on his lonely night ride, he wrote in his *Memories of Forty-*

eight Years' Service, "It ought to have been a very jumpy ride, for I was entirely alone and the country was wild and new to me, and the road little better than a track; but pride that I had been selected to carry an important despatch and the valour of ignorance (for I only realised next day that the country was infested with hostile Zulus) carried me along without a thought of danger."

Smith-Dorrien reached Rorke's Drift about 6 A.M., giving the order to Capt. George Shepstone, who told him that Colonel Durnford had left an hour earlier to bring up additional wagons. Lieutenant Henderson was sent after him, and on receiving the despatch Durnford remarked, "Ah, just what I expected; we are to go at once. The General has gone out to attack an impi." He got his troops moving, and at 7:30 A.M. he marched for Isandhlwana, encountering Lieutenant Chard on his way back to the Drift, where he was stationed. Chard told Durnford that the Zulus were "showing on the crests of distant hills," and that several parties were working round to the left, preparing, perhaps, to make a dash on the Drift or to take the camp from the rear. Smith-Dorrien, eager to get back to Isandhlwana, where, he felt, a fight was imminent, borrowed some revolver ammunition and rode in that direction, hearing the sound of heavy firing in the distance.

At the camp the advance force fell in before dawn. The 2nd Battalion 24th Regiment had been ordered to be under arms by daybreak. The men, roused silently and without light, were unable to find all their personal belongings in the dark. They were ordered to turn out in light marching order, taking only their ammunition bags containing seventy rounds, their haversacks with one day's rations, and their water bottles. Bandmaster Bullard and his four drummer boys were ordered to remain in camp, but at the last moment these bandsmen, who also acted as stretcher bearers, were told to join the advance force with every available stretcher and two ambulance wagons. They were to owe their lives to this change of plan. The colours of the 2nd Battalion were left in camp, as experience had proved it was impossible for a regiment to carry its colours while bush fighting or scaling krantzes.

At 4:30 A.M. Colonel Glyn led out his force, consisting of six companies of the 2nd Battalion 24th Regiment, the mounted infantry, four guns of Colonel Harness's battery and the Native Pioneers, leaving behind, under Colonel Pulleine's command, a "caretaker force," as Smith-Dorrien named it, consisting of five companies of the 1st Battalion 24th Regiment (16 officers and 403 men), one company of the 2nd Battalion (5 officers and 178 men), two heavy guns, 2 artillery officers and 70 artillerymen, 20 Natal Carabineers, 31 mounted police, and four companies of the native contingent. The forty-five wagons that had been unloaded and were due to be returned to Rorke's Drift for further supplies were ordered to stay in camp, as the force remaining was too small to furnish the necessary escort. But no attempt was made to form them into a laager, their conductors being ordered only to yoke up the oxen.

Lord Chelmsford felt confident that he had taken all necessary steps to ensure the safety of the camp, as he set out at break of day to attack the Zulus that had been spotted by Major Dartnell the night before. At 6 A.M. his forces reached the position occupied by Major Dartnell—a ridge about ten miles southeast of the camp, to the right of the conspicuous Isipezi Hill, whose conical mound rose in the centre of the plain. The hills ahead were still blanketed with mist, and nothing could be seen. Then, as the moisture dissolved in the heat of the sun, several Zulu scouts were discerned on the crests, protecting, it was thought, the impi that had been seen the night before. Lord Chelmsford ordered an advance, sending out two forces to probe the hills in front of his men.

Colonel Russell, in command of the mounted infantry, taking with him the four guns and six companies of the 24th Regiment, proceeded up the valley ahead, while Major Dartnell, with his Natal Carabineers and Mounted Police, was attempting to get between the position where he had seen the Zulus the night before and Matyana's stronghold. Reaching the crest of the ridge after a hard pull up, Dartnell's men saw a number of the Zulus moving up to occupy the ridge. Realizing they had been spotted, and were in danger of being outflanked by Russell's force, the Zulus ran down the hillside, taking refuge in caves and amongst rocks, from where it took Russell's men three hours to evict them. Lieutenant Harford distinguished himself greatly in the action by crawling into a dark crevasse and shooting two Zulus and taking a third prisoner. All together eighty Zulus were killed.

Leaving Russell to mop up the rest of the enemy, Dartnell rode in pursuit of a body of mounted Zulus, commanded, it was learned later, by Matyana himself, who jeered at the British when they fired ineffectively at 800 yards' range, until two of their warriors were killed by chance shots. The Zulus mounted their horses hurriedly and galloped up the hill as hard as they could, pursued by the Natal Carabineers, who, reducing the distance to 600 yards, inflicted a number of casualties. Matyana was nearly caught by Captain Shepstone, who chased him for miles, until the chieftain, seeing himself in danger of capture, abandoned his horse and hid in a rocky krantz.

All efforts to make contact with the main body of Zulus proved fruitless, for, as the British advanced, the enemy fell back, abandoning strong positions and showing no intention of allowing the invaders to engage them in battle. This retreat of the Zulus led Lord Chelmsford to call them "cowardly." Actually the Zulus were following a plan whereby Chelmsford's force would be drawn farther and farther from their camp—a stratagem that Lord Chelmsford did not suspect until it was too late. There was no Zulu impi "over the hill" as Lord Chelmsford had imagined: the impi, 20,000 strong, lay hidden five miles to the north of the camp from which he had marched so blithely away that morning. As he was soon to learn, but not to appreciate, its right horn was quietly moving behind the Ngutu Hills to outflank the camp at Isandhlwana.

Lord Chelmsford called a halt for breakfast at 9 A.M. While he and his staff officers were offsaddled, a mounted-police orderly came spurring in with a message from Colonel Pulleine, timed at 8:05 A.M., which stated, "Report just come in that Zulus are advancing in force from left of camp," and he requested the General to return at once with all the forces at his command.

Chelmsford was in a dilemma. He was now twelve miles from Isandhlwana; it would take his troops two to three hours' hard riding and marching to get back. His objective was to push forward to the next campsite, making sure that there was no strong body of the enemy to hinder the advance of the remainder of his troops from Isandhlwana. He felt confident that Pulleine and Durnford, who must by now be nearing Isandhlwana, could defend the camp from any number of Zulus who might have got round to the north unobserved. They hardly could be many, for there had been no hint of their presence in that vicinity the night before. He ignored the warnings he had received of the Zulus' amazing mobility and ability at concealment. What should he do? Continue his advance or hurry back to the camp on what might prove to be

[63]

a fool's errand? The staff stood silent as the General paced up and down.

Then, suddenly, he saw a way out of the difficulty. Standing in the background was his A.D.C., Lt. Berkeley Milne, of the Naval Brigade, a large telescope under his arm. Climb to the top of the ridge and take a look at the camp, Lord Chelmsford ordered. Milne, later a distinguished admiral, ascended the hill and trained his powerful telescope on the camp. After a searching inspection he came down to report, "No sign of the enemy at Isandhlwana." He had noticed nothing unusual, he said, except that "the cattle had been driven into the camp close around the tents."

Lord Chelmsford's anxieties were allayed. He ordered the advance to continue, and as a half-measure he despatched Commander Browne and his native contingent back to the camp, ordering him to search the dongas on the way for lurking Zulus.

The General had made the wrong decision. The last moment when he might have staved off the impending disaster by a speedy return to the camp had passed. The fatal question had been posed, the fatal answer given. Lord Chelmsford sent Milne back up the hill to watch the camp.

The white officers of the native corps, men born and bred in Natal, were worried, for they knew from their experience of native warfare that the bringing of cattle into camp was the first sign of danger. Nor were the men of the 24th Regiment happy about their general's decision after they had talked with the mounted messenger from the camp. Colonel Degacher, commander of the 2nd Battalion, noticing that the news he communicated to the men caused great excitement, asked the cause and was told, "He says, sir, that the camp is being surrounded and attacked." This was startling intelligence; but as

[64]

there was no stir among the staff and no sign of anything un-usual, the men were told not to let the police orderly chaff them, since if what he said were true, "we should all be march-ing back as fast as we could." The men, however, were much impressed, believing that the orderly had seen more on his way than was reported in his despatch.

What had caused Colonel Pulleine to inform his chief that the Zulus were in force on the left of the camp? How far was he justified in requesting the General to return at once? On paper, Pulleine's position was a strong one, if he stayed in the camp, as he had been ordered to do. He had plenty of am-munition, two field guns and six hundred redcoats armed with breech-loading rifles effective up to a range of 600 yards. He had a force of native auxiliaries, one in ten armed with rifles and the rest with assegais. The camp would soon be re-inforced by Durnford and his 450 natives, making a total force of 1,700 men. At the rear of the camp stood 150 wagons, which could be turned into a laager at short notice. Scouts and vedettes posted at 2,000 yards' range guarded against sur-prise. This surely was a force strong enough to defend the camp against no matter how many Zulus armed chiefly with close-combat weapons, and possessing only a few guns.

There were several "but's" and "if's." While the plain in front of the camp was open to the east and south, the view to the north and northeast was obscured by the Ngutu Hills, behind which the enemy could advance unseen, and the rear of the camp could be turned from the north. The position was a strong one if, and only if, the defence forces were kept together. Yet, both Pulleine and Durnford, when he arrived, extended the line. No attempt was made to laager the wagons, and worst of all, no ammunition supply to forward troops was organised. But at 8:05 A.M., when Pulleine sent the despatch rider galloping to Lord Chelmsford, there was apparently no great cause for alarm.

At 8 A.M. a report came to Pulleine from a mounted patrol on the hills about 2,000 yards to the northeast that three columns of Zulus were approaching along the valley below. On receipt of this startling information Pulleine despatched the mounted policeman to find Lord Chelmsford and called his men to arms. Within a few minutes they were drawn up in front of the camp. The Zulus seen by the patrol soon dispersed. For an hour nothing happened, then at 9 A.M. those in camp saw a mass of Zulus marching westward along the crest of the hills to the northeast, but they, too, soon passed out of sight. There was no particular cause for alarm; the sight of bodies of Zulus was to be expected; the General had gone out to make contact with a large body believed to be lying southeast of the camp. Pulleine ordered his men to withdraw to their tents and stand at ease. The panic was over for the moment. He did not know that his outposts had seen the right horn of the Zulu impi, which was taking up position to throw itself on the camp at lightning speed, not that day but at dawn next morning—an attack now to be precipitated by Colonel Durnford's misguided advance east of the camp.

Unable to come to grips with the elusive Zulus, and satisfied there was no cause for anxiety about the camp at Isandhlwana, Lord Chelmsford pushed on to select the next campsite by the Amangene stream. Capt. Alan Gardner was sent back to the camp, the bearer of an order to Pulleine to send out the camp equipment belonging to the advance force. Three officers who had come out for the ride, Maj. Stuart Smith, Royal Artillery, and Lieutenants Griffith and Dyer of the 24th Regiment, accompanied Gardner.

Colonel Glyn led his men towards the new campsite, and

Colonel Harness, some distance in the rear, was ordered to take his guns by a circuitous route, avoiding the rough ground over which the infantry and cavalry could march and ride with ease. It was now 10:30 A.M., and the day was becoming uncomfortably hot. Lieutenant Milne was recalled from his hilltop, from where he had been watching the camp through his telescope for over an hour, again reporting that he could see nothing unusual. The sun, he said, was shining brightly on the tents, amongst which he could see people moving about. Everything seemed quite normal, as in fact it then was. Lord Chelmsford was reassured. If the camp had been threatened, the tents would have been thrown down, according to standing orders.

At Isandhlwana wagon conductor J. A. Brickhill was busy at the rear of the camp, supervising the yoking of the teams of oxen to the forty-five wagons he expected to take back to Rorke's Drift for more supplies, when he saw Durnford's Basuto horsemen winding up the road from Rorke's Drift. A welcome addition to the camp's meagre forces, he thought, as he signalled their approach to Colonel Pulleine, who had returned to his tent after the morning alert. Standing on the neck between Isandhlwana Mount and Stoney Hill to the south, Brickhill listened to the sound of distant volley firing, which he placed in the direction taken by the General—clear proof, he thought, that the advance force was engaged with the impi it had gone out to find.

Colonel Durnford reached the camp with his 450 natives and mounted Basutos and rocket battery at 9:30 A.M., eager for a fight. He rode at once to Colonel Pulleine's tent. There are various versions of their conversation, which, after the battle when blame was being apportioned, became magnified into a row. "High words," it was said, "were exchanged," an occurrence completely denied by eyewitness testimony.

According to Lieutenant Cockrane, Durnford's staff officer, his chief asked for the latest information, and Pulleine told him that columns of Zulus had been seen on the hills to the north, one moving to the left rear of the camp, another in the direction taken by the General. He estimated the enemy's strength at from 400 to 600 men. The manner of the officers to one another was perfectly genial and courteous. To Durnford, Pulleine said, "I'm sorry you have come, as you are senior to me and will of course take command"; to which Durnford replied, "I am not going to interfere with you. I am not going to remain in camp." He said he was going out to intercept the Zulu column reported having been seen in the General's direction, and he asked Pulleine to spare him two companies of the 24th Regiment to strengthen his force. Pulleine demurred, saying he did not feel justified in sending away any men, as his orders were "to defend the camp." "But the Zulus are retiring," urged Durnford. "Very well, if you order it, I will give them," Pulleine replied. But Durnford refused to take a high hand. If he got into any difficulty he would ask for them again, he said. Lieutenant Smith-Dorrien's recollection of the conversation was similar to Cockrane's. Durnford wished to go out and attack the Zulus; Pulleine argued that his orders were to defend the camp. Mr. Brickhill states that Colonel Durnford, hearing that Zulus had been seen, proposed to go out and attack them, and he asked Pulleine to lend him two white companies. Pulleine protested that such a course was contrary to the written instructions he had received, which he fetched from his tent and read to Colonel Durnford. Durnford then said, "Well, my idea is, that wherever Zulus appear, we ought to attack. I will go alone, but, remember, if I get into difficulties, I shall rely on you to support me."

Lieutenant Cockrane said that while Durnford and Pulleine were conferring, reports were coming in constantly. Some of them noted that "the enemy are in force behind the hills to the left"; "the enemy are in three columns"; "the columns are separating and moving to the left rear and one towards the General"; "the enemy are retiring in every direction." This last message was brought by a man not in uniform.

Thus, according to the testimony of eyewitnesses, Durnford did not actually assume command of the camp at Isandhlwana, although it was recognised that as senior officer he was in command of the operations centered on the camp. Pulleine, it might be said, was left in local command. Neither he nor Durnford gave any orders to strengthen the camp's defences by laagering the wagons or entrenching, and it appears that apart from his own disastrous movement to the east, Durnford, according to both Cockrane and Captain Essex, gave orders before he went out that resulted in the further widening of the camp's perimeter. He sent native scouts to the top of Isandhlwana Mount, from where a wide view could be obtained, which Pulleine apparently had omitted to do. He then ordered two companies of natives and a troop of Basuto horse, under Captain Barton and Lieutenant Raw, with whom his political agent, Captain Shepstone, went, to reconnoitre the hills to the north of the camp. Not satisfied with these precautions, Durnford despatched one company of Pulleine's 1st Battalion of the 24th, commanded by Lt. George Cavaye, without, as far as we know, Pulleine protesting, on piquet to the hills to the north, about 2,000 yards distant, to prevent the Zulus from moving westward in the direction of Rorke's Drift—a manoeuvre that was to lead in an hour's time to incalculable repercussions when Pulleine sought to reinforce Cavaye's company, thereby further weakening his defences.

Durnford himself now moved out of the camp southeastwards into the plain with most of his native troops and mounted Basutos and Major Russell's rocket battery. His quite laudable but ill-advised intention was to protect Lord Chelmsford's rear and his line of retreat from the Zulu column, which he imagined was marching to join the impi with which the General was supposed to be engaged. His move was a fatal one, for it led to a further scattering of the camp's defences; it left a thousand-yard gap on the camp's right, and it precipitated the Zulu attack that would otherwise have been delayed until the next morning. Durnford led his men in the direction of the conspicuous Isipezi Hill on the spur of the range, about a mile and a half from the camp.

Durnford left behind him a camp ill prepared for what was to follow. It was now 11 A.M.; the day was hot and sultry; the sun shone brightly on the tents, as Lieutenant Milne observed from twelve miles away through his telescope. All was quiet. The cooks were busy preparing the men's dinner; the soldiers relaxed in their tents. Over the hills five miles in front of Durnford's men the Zulu impi squatted on its haunches in an immense half-circle—performing the ceremonies that preceded a battle still unperformed, awaiting the rise of the new moon to herald the propitious time for the attack on the white invaders of their land.

Everyone in camp, said Captain Essex, felt that the enemy had no intention of advancing during the day, but might possibly be expected to attack during the night.

7

THE IMPI

THE INCIDENTS of the battle that are now about to be joined were separated in place and time. The battle of Isandhlwana stretched at its outset over an area of several square miles; at its conclusion it had become contracted to a few square yards. Of those directly involved only a few men survived to tell the story, not of the battle itself, but what he experienced personally. There was no William Howard Russell or Richard Harding Davis to paint a picture in words. Orders, reports and documents were lost in the sack of Isandhlwana camp, in and around which on January 22, 1879, 1,500 British soldiers and their native allies, and some 3,000 Zulus died. But we do have the observations of war correspondents Norris Newman and Archibald Forbes and war artist Melton Prior, after their visits to the scene of the disaster some months later.

Colonel Durnford and his mounted Basutos, riding in the direction of the conical hill, soon outstripped Russell's rocket battery and its infantry escort, which included three men of the 24th Regiment. As they mounted the plateau about three miles from the camp, the Basutos spotted a herd of cattle and

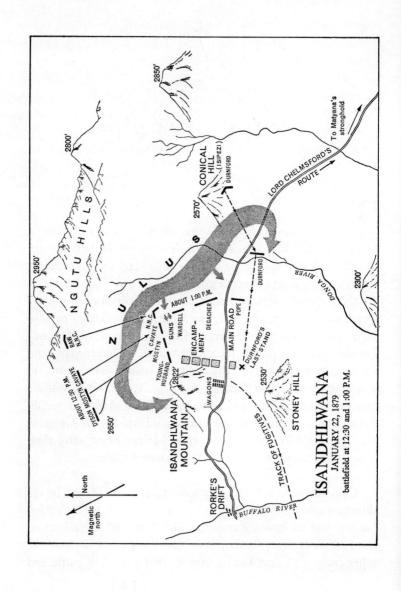

ISANDHLWANA
JANUARY 22, 1879
battlefield at 12:30 and 1:00 P.M.

gave chase. This brought them to the brink of a valley; below them squatted a vast mass of Zulus in battle array, and another large body was moving away to the north.

Seeing that the carefully guarded secret of their presence close to the camp had been discovered, the Zulus sprang to arms, their Umcityu regiment of young men, heedless of orders, rushing towards the startled Basutos. The assault on the camp, planned for dawn next day, had to be launched at once, saw the Zulu general Dabulamanzi,* Cetewayo's half-brother. Into the battle he threw his regiments: the Nodwengu, the Nokenke, the Mbonambi, the Nokobamakosi, the Tulwana, the Qikazi, the Umcityu. The Zulu right horn circled round to the north of the camp, the centre converged on its north and east, and the left horn engaged Durnford's forces.

Durnford's unlucky manoeuvre had stirred up the wasps' nest. Pursued by the Umcityu and the Nokobamakosi Regiments, the Basutos retreated, occasionally halting to fire their rifles. Trooper Whitelaw of the Natal Carabineers galloped ahead to warn the Colonel—a warning he did not now need, for the Zulus were pouring over the hill in perfect alignment. On the left Russell's rocket battery opened up, but his men succeeded in getting only one rocket away before a party of the enemy, emerging suddenly from a ravine, pounced upon them, stampeding the mules and scattering the escorting natives commanded by Captain Nourse. In the hand-to-hand fighting, Major Russell, five of his white men and most of the mule drivers were killed. Privates Grant, Trainer and Johnson of the 24th succeeded in reaching Colonel Durnford, whom they told of Russell's death. "Go back and fetch his body," ordered Durnford. By the time Durnford could hurry to the spot, all

* Some Zulu sources state that the supreme command was in the hands of a general named Ntshingwayo.

[73]

was over. The battery was out of action and had to be abandoned, only Captain Nourse being saved. Galloping back to his Basutos, Durnford threw them in a skirmishing line and continued his retreat, halting and opening fire wherever the ground was favourable, keeping up a steady fire for two miles, disputing every yard of the ground, the Zulus constantly endeavouring to outflank him. At length he reached a dry watercourse about 800 yards in front of the camp, where, reinforced by thirty mounted colonists under Captain Bradstreet, his troops made a stand. All this had taken nearly an hour, and by the time Durnford reached the donga, the camp itself was under savage attack.

After Durnford left the camp, Pulleine had become uneasy. His eyes kept straying to the hills to the north, the camp's blind spot, from which an assault might be expected to come. He comforted himself with the thought that Lieutenant Cavaye with his company of the 24th and Lieutenant Raw with his Basutos, both in the hills to the north, would give timely warning of trouble. It was now just past noon, and Pulleine was still unaware that Durnford had stumbled upon the Zulu impi and set it in motion. His first intimation of trouble came with the sound of firing from the heights to the north, where Lieutenant Cavaye was posted.

The complete surprise achieved by the Zulus can be gathered from a letter written three days after the attack by Captain Essex, a transport officer, who amazingly survived not only the disaster at Isandhlwana but two British defeats in the subsequent war with the Boers. Essex wrote:

I had been present all this time but wishing to write some letters, and thinking everything was now quiet, I went to my tent and sat down, and was seen too soon busy with my papers. About noon a sergeant came into my tent and told me that firing was to be heard behind the hill where the company of the 1st battalion 24th had been sent. I had my glasses over my shoulder, and I thought I might as well take my revolver, but did not trouble to put on my sword, as I thought nothing of the matter, and expected to be back in half an hour to complete my letters.

On the high ground to the north, Lieutenant Raw had advanced three miles from the camp when his forward troop sighted a party of Zulus driving away a herd of cattle. Raw was ordered by Captain Shepstone to give chase. Galloping forward over the crest, he spied a huge impi in the valley below, its centre advancing directly on the camp, its right horn pushing up the valley towards the camp's rear. As the horn began to descend from the valley, it came under fire from Cavaye's company at 800 yards' range, but it continued to stream westwards on its encircling movement. On seeing this, Raw ordered a retreat, sending Shepstone galloping back to camp with the news that the whole Zulu army was advancing to attack it.

Shepstone pulled up at Colonel Pulleine's tent simultaneously with Captain Gardner, who had come from Lord Chelmsford with the order to send on the advance force's tents. Shepstone was quite out of breath, and Gardner got his word in first. Pulleine read the General's letter aloud; it was an order to strike camp and come on with all speed, leaving a sufficient guard behind to protect such stores as could not be moved without delay. Captain Shepstone then interrupted to say, "I am not an alarmist, sir, but the Zulus are in such black masses over there, such long black lines, that you will have to give us all the assistance you can. They are now fast driving our men this way." "I assure you that affairs are very serious," he emphasized. Captain Gardner told Colonel Pulleine (who, reported Mr. Brickhill, seemed thoroughly nonplussed as to what he ought to do): "Under the circumstances I should advise your disobeying the General's order, for the present at any rate. The General knows nothing of this. He is only think-ing of the cowardly way in which the Zulus are running before our troops over yonder." With the Colonel's consent, Gardner dispatched a message to Lord Chelmsford advising, "Our left attacked by about 10,000 of the enemy," and adding that Cap-tain Shepstone had come in asking for reinforcements, because all his Basutos were falling back, and because "the whole force at the camp turned out and fighting about one mile to the left flank, cannot move camp at present."

At first Colonel Pulleine refused to send out reinforcements to help Raw and Cavaye. His forces were already too far ex-tended, he replied to Shepstone's urgent entreaties. Then he agreed to support them with two companies of the 24th, those commanded by Captains William Mostyn and R. Young-husband. The bugles sounded the alarm and the troops turned out of their tents, many of them half dressed. Captain Mostyn, accompanied by Lieutenant Dyson, hurried up the hills to the camp's left. Captain Younghusband took his company out in support, remaining nearer the camp.

The three other British companies Pulleine drew up facing northeast, with the two guns on their flanks, a position he changed subsequently; for half an hour later the two guns were on the left of the soldiers, about half a mile from the camp, facing north.

Nobody was left in the camp itself, except the servants, hospital orderlies, bandsmen–stretcher bearers, dismounted men and wagon conductors, who, although armed with rifles and therefore available for the defence of the camp, were too few to resist with any chance of success should the Zulus rush round the rear of the scattered fighting line.

The positions shortly after noon were approximately as follows: three troops of natives (Lieutenant Raw) and two companies of the 24th (Cavaye and Mostyn) were extended on the hills about a mile to the left of the camp, with Captain Younghusband positioned somewhere outside the camp in their support. Captains W. Degacher's and G. V. Wardell's companies of the 1st Battalion of the 24th, and Lt. Charles Pope's company of the 2nd Battalion, were extended in front of the camp, facing east, about a mile from the tents, the two guns probably being on their left, and flanked by the contingent of Natal natives. Colonel Pulleine and his adjutant, Lieutenant Melville, rode up and down behind the line. Thus most of the camp's troops were deployed facing north and northeast of the camp. Somewhere on the right a force of Natal Mounted Police was drawn up between the camp and Colonel Durnford, who had by now reached the donga in front of the camp, where he was making a stand with his force of native levies and Basuto horsemen.

Colonel Pulleine had one half of his own battalion 1,000 yards from the camp, through the necessity of supporting a company that ought not to have been sent out. Masses of Zulus, belonging to the Nokenke Regiment, who had swarmed quickly up the hill, were now running halfway down the steep slope towards the camp and working round to the west. The British companies on the hills were firing volleys, and Cavaye's ammunition was running low.

The Zulu attack began to develop rapidly, the regiments assuming their traditional formation with a solid mass in the centre and enveloping "horns" thrown out to right and left. Thus, whilst the centre regiments, afterwards identified as the

Umcityu right centre and Nokenke left centre, moved directly upon the camp, those on the left, afterwards identified as the Mbonambi and Nokobamakosi Regiments, worked southwestwards in order to turn the British right flank; and the right horn, afterwards identified as the Undi Corps, pursued a route to the west of Isandhlwana Mount with a view toward completing the circle round its southern slopes.

Mr. Brickhill, the wagon conductor who also acted as interpreter to Colonel Pulleine, had been listening to Colonel Pulleine's conversation with Captains Gardner and Shepstone, and hurriedly mounted his horse and rode about the camp, vainly hoping to find a weapon and join in the fight. He was disappointed and took himself to a commanding position in the rear of the tents, from where he could see the whole Zulu force spreading out in battle array and pouring down the slopes of the hills, pushing before them the Basutos and redcoats in whose support the two fieldpieces were firing furiously. The rest of the infantry was drawn up in a thin red line about a mile to the left and to the front of the tents.

Mostyn's and Dyson's men had scarcely climbed the heights, where they extended to Cavaye's left, when both companies and Raw's Basutos were compelled by the Zulus to abandon their positions and retreat, the Basutos riding down the slope, to find their retreat threatened by a strong party of Zulus confronting them. But, keeping up a resolute fire, Raw held them in check, and the Basutos were able to withdraw onto the the camp. The retreat of these forces was supported by Captain Younghusband's company and by the two camp guns, which threw shrapnel into the dense masses of Zulus, some of whom were now only 800 yards from the camp. The retreat had the effect of uniting the troops originally sent out to the northern heights with those stationed in front of the camp, a line being formed facing roughly northeast and east, the most vulnerable section of which, the position on the apex of the triangle, was guarded by the native contingent—men who could hardly be expected to put up the same resistance as British regulars.

The Zulu army was steadily and inexorably closing in from almost every direction, and although tremendous punishment was inflicted on its densely packed ranks by accurate rifle fire supported by the two guns, there were always others to take the place of those who fell. British casualties had so far been light, for the Zulus had not as yet got to close quarters with their assegais, and their firing was wild.

It was now one o'clock. Looking down from his position at the rear of the camp Mr. Brickhill saw that the plain in front was "black with Zulus." The sun, he said, was shining brightly, the Zulu spears glinting in its rays.

Two minutes later, at 1:02 P.M. the sunlight began to fade. During the next three hours, while the battle of Isandhlwana was being fought, the moon passed betwen the earth and the sun, causing a partial eclipse.

8

THE GALLANT 24TH

WHILE THE CAMP was being rushed from the north and east, and the Zulu right horn was sweeping round to take it in the rear, Colonel Durnford stood at the donga on the right front holding the Zulu left horn at bay, 600 yards in advance of Lieutenant Pope's company of the 24th. "This gully," says Mr. Brickhill, the wagon conductor, "the mounted men held most tenaciously, every shot appearing to take effect. A thousand Zulu dead must have lain between the conical hill and the gully." These bodies looked just like peppercorns, says the metaphor-minded wagon conductor.

Jabez, one of Colonel Durnford's Basutos, who had been a faithful follower of Durnford's since the Bushman's River Pass affair, where he had been wounded, gave the following account:

> At last we came to a bad stony place and a little stream quite close to the camp. Here we made a long stand, firing incessantly. The Colonel rode up and down our line continually, encouraging us all—talking and even laughing with us—"Fire, my boys!" "Well done, my boys!" he cried. Some of us did not like his exposing

himself so much, and wanted him to keep behind, but he laughed at us, and said, "All right, nonsense." He was very calm and cheerful all the time. There were not very many of us, but because of the way in which we were handled by our leader we were enough to stop the Zulus on that side for a long time. We could have carried him off with us safely enough at this time, only we knew him too well to try. But we now say, "If we had known what would happen, we would have seized him and bound him, no matter if he had fought us for doing so, as he certainly would; no matter if he had killed some of us, we would have saved his life, for he was our master." Now we say that we shall always remember him by his commanding voice, and the way in which he gave us all some of his own spirit as he went along our line that day, and those amongst us who had not served under him before, as I had, say, "Why did we not know him sooner?" We see also that but for him we should all have died that day.

Jabez said afterwards that in all the years through which he had followed the Colonel, and watched his sad face, he had never seen him look so bright and happy—never seen his face shine and his eyes brighten—as during the last fight in the donga nearest the camp, when he knew for certain that he would die.

Lieutenant Davis, who was with Durnford and miraculously survived, stated that his chief stood up to call to his men, "Let the enemy come a little closer, then fire and keep firing. Keep them at a distance of two hundred yards."

Mehlokazulu, Sirayo's son whose rash act had provided Frere with the excuse he was looking for to attack Cetewayo, commanded a wing of the Nkobamakosi Regiment that attacked the donga; he said after the war was over:

They poured into us a regular hail of bullets, which temporarily stopped our advance. They had taken their horses into the donga with them, so that all we could see to fire at was a line of white helmets. The firing got more furious until it forced us to retire. We kept lying down and rising again. When we saw we could not drive them out, we extended our horn to the bottom of the donga, the lower part crossing and advancing on the camp in a semicircle. When the mounted men saw this, they came out of the donga, and galloped to the camp. Our horn suffered a great deal, both from the mounted men and a cross fire from the soldiers.

Durnford's ammunition was running low. He had repeatedly sent back to the camp for more, but, according to Captain Barton, who commanded one troop of the native contingent, he was refused, because all the ammunition was needed for the British infantry. Jabez says that the men in the donga continued firing until their last cartridge was gone. Colonel Durnford then ordered a retreat to the camp. On the way back the native troops, losing heart, began to slip away in twos and threes, seeking safety in flight before the road to Rorke's Drift was closed. Nearing the camp Durnford met Captain Essex, who told him of the threat to the left and rear. Realising the danger of the camp's being taken from behind, Durnford told Essex "to take some of [his] men to that part of the field and endeavour to hold the enemy in check." Durnford himself made for the rising ground between Stoney Hill and Isandhlwana Mount, where he was joined by a party of Colonial Horse.

Lieutenant Cockrane, observing the Zulus massing in front of him, pointed it out to Colonel Durnford and asked if he should send an orderly to call it to the attention of the artillery. Durnford told him, "No, they may not attend to him; you had better go yourself." Cockrane rode off. He never saw his chief again. Nor did Jabez, whom Durnford sent into the camp to try to find ammunition. Both owed their lives to the chance errands on which they were sent.

While Durnford was retreating from the donga to Stoney Hill, the main battle for the camp was being fought and lost. But disaster was not inevitable, even at this late stage. Younghusband's, Mostyn's and Cavaye's companies of the 24th Foot had made a successful withdrawal to the north front of the camp. On their right, at the corner of the rectangle as the line turned eastwards, stood the native contingent, and next to them the two field guns commanded by Maj. Stuart Smith and Lieutenant Curling. Then in order, facing eastwards, came two companies of the 1st Battalion 24th Regiment commanded by Captains Degacher and Wardell, and one company of the 2nd Battalion, led by Lieutenant Pope. Each company comprised about a hundred men and noncommissioned officers, grouped under Lieutenants Francis Porteous, Edgar Anstey, Neville Coghill, J. P. Daly, Hodson, C. J. Atkinson, Frederick Goodwin-Austen, E. H. Dyer and T. L. S. Griffith. In advance of Pope's company was Durnford's force, now retiring to take position between that company and the right rear of the camp. The defence line stretched for 3,000 yards, but there were many gaps, the widest and most dangerous being the thousand-yard space between Pope and Durnford. The weakest point in the line, the corner of the rectangle on the northeast, was defended by the native troops, only one in ten armed with a rifle, the rest with assegais, men without experience of battle who had been brought up on stories of the terrible ferocity of the Zulu warriors, their own cousins.

There were two other fatal weaknesses; one was that the defence line, overstretched, with yawning gaps, was situated 1,000 yards in advance of the tents and wagons pitched and standing on the slope immediately below Isandhlwana Mount.

[83]

If, on the first hint of the Zulu assault, Colonel Pulleine had tightened his line and withdrawn it closer to the tents, his men, British and native, could have presented a compact half-circle, with the Mount at their back, and might have succeeded in throwing back the Zulu hordes. As it was, they nearly did so. That they failed was due to the second, and most fatal, weakness: there was no organised supply of ammunition to the firing line. When some ammunition was brought up by the bandsmen, it was found that the boxes were screwed down, and there were no screwdrivers with which to open them. (When such appliances were asked for while the 24th Regiment was still in Natal, the answer had been: "The articles applied for are not in store. . . . However useful and necessary such appliances may be in European warfare, it is not expected that they will be required in a war such as the troops are about to enter upon.")

Lieutenant Smith-Dorrien tried to organise a supply for the companies of the 1st Battalion 24th Regiment by breaking boxes open, but he was told by Quartermaster Bloomfield of the 2nd Battalion, "For heaven's sake don't take that, man, for it belongs to our Battalion." "Hang it all, you don't want a requisition now, do you?" was all that the exasperated young officer could reply, pointing to the hordes of Zulus rushing at the camp.

Some 1,700 men in all—white and black—including Durnford's command, the officers' servants, camp followers and transport drivers, stood facing the onslaught of 20,000 Zulus, flushed with their initial victory over Durnford, charging towards the camp in the face of a hailstorm of bullets. The Zulu warriors came on with reckless bravery. Each warrior was an awe-inspiring sight, every man an athlete, strong and tall, naked except for a loincloth, colourful in the ostrich plumes adorning his shoulders and legs, bare-footed, clutching a short stabbing assegai in one hand, in the other a four-foot ox-skin shield and several throwing assegais. All the warriors were of ferocious countenance, and, emboldened by the illustrious record of their glorious military past and enraged by the sight of the invaders of their homeland, they were a sight before which even the strongest might quail.

Moving steadily from the northeast, in a loose but deep formation of horseshoe shape, the Zulu right horn fell on the left of the British camp, the central mass converged on its front, and the left horn pushed Durnford back and threw itself into the thousand-yard gap between him and Lieutenant Pope. The defenders could now see the enormous force of their adversaries, who outnumbered them by twelve to one, everywhere pressing forward regardless of the heaviest losses, the horseshoe flattening out into a gigantic crescent.

Some attempt was made at this stage to organise a supply of ammunition, several officers, including Smith-Dorrien and Essex, rushing back to the wagons. Wally Erskine, a lieutenant acting as captain of native levies, did not even have a rifle. Galloping back to fetch one, he met his superior officer, Captain Stafford, who ordered him to the rear of the camp to try and organise a resistance on the neck. To these chance moves all three officers owed their lives. About this time Colonel Pulleine despatched Lieutenant Andrews of the Native Pioneer Corps and Private Edwards of the Buffs, to ride to Rorke's Drift to give the alarm, a message that was delivered, but not by either of these men.

For the first time in their history, the Zulus faced the disciplined volley firing of a British regiment of the line, an experience the survivors never forgot. "It was terrible," one warrior told a white man afterwards. The fire of the field guns was less destructive, for the quick-witted Zulus learned that the movement of the gunners standing clear heralded a shell, and they avoided injury by throwing themselves to the ground. "The cannon didn't do much damage. It only killed four men in our regiment. The shots went over us," one warrior recalled months later. Others described the bullets whizzing around them as like "the passing of a storm of bees." "We tossed our heads from side to side and let the bullets pass," stated one imaginative young Zulu.

Smith-Dorrien, who dashed about the camp to where the fight was thickest, recalls that the Zulus came on steadily towards the British line, giving vent to no loud war cry but advancing with a low, musical, murmuring noise that gave him the impression of a gigantic swarm of bees approaching nearer and nearer. The companies of the 24th were formed in line, the front ranks kneeling, firing volley after volley into the dense black mass. These men, Smith-Dorrien says, were "no boy recruits but war-worn matured men, mostly with beards, veterans of a long campaign in Cape Colony against the Kaffirs, where they had carried everything before them. Possessed of splendid discipline and sure of success, they held their ground, making every shot tell into the serried black mass before them." "The men were laughing and chatting and thought they were giving the blacks an awful hammering," recalled another officer. So terrible was their fire that when the Zulu army was still some 200 yards off, it wavered.

For fifteen minutes the Zulus were held in check by the withering volley firing of the redcoats and by the guns, firing grape, canister and shot, which ploughed great lanes in the Zulu ranks, now too tightly packed for the warriors to jump for cover. As the gaps opened up, the were immediately filled by other warriors.

[86]

Then the volley firing of the 24th petered out. With thousands of rounds of ammunition in the rear, there were none on the firing line. The cartridges carried by each man had been used up. After the war the Zulus told Smith-Dorrien that the fire was too hot for them and that they were on the verge of retreat when it slackened. A warrior of the Nkobamakosi Regiment said they were repulsed three times and were able to press forward only when another regiment came up to support them. The men of his regiment fell in great heaps, he said, and the hill down which they charged was covered with dead.

Then, suddenly, a black warrior leaped to the front, crying with a great voice, "Cetewayo has not ordered us to run away," and like a mass of black panthers the Zulu hordes again sprang forward.

With the failure of ammunition in the firing line, there was no hope. The soldiers stood helpless, their last cartridge spent, 600 men armed with bayonets, a thin red line tipped with steel, withstanding the surging charge of thousands of the finest close-combat warriors the world has ever seen. The evidence of the dead told one unvarying tale of groups of men fighting back to back until the last cartridge was gone. Zulu witnesses, after the war, all told the same story: "At first we could make no way against these soldiers, but suddenly they ceased to fire; then we came round them and threw our spears until we had killed them all."

All along the line the Zulus rushed in. Just in front of the companies of the 24th, at the corner of the dangerous rectangle, stood the native contingent. At 60 yards' range the Zulus stopped to fling their assegais. Up to then they had advanced in utter silence. Now from the lips of thousands of throats rose a ferocious, exultant war cry, heralding the final charge. "Si-gi-di," screamed the Zulus, mad with battle lust.

This proved too much for the Natal natives. They blanched and bolted, leaving a huge gap through which the Zulus burst. In an instant all was confusion; the companies of the 24th on either side were outflanked. The two guns, after having discharged a few rounds into the swirling mass at point-blank range, were limbered up and dashed back towards the tents.

Before the men of the 24th had time to rally, the Zulus were among them. Mehlokazulu described their end.

> Some of us threw assegais at them, but we did not come within reach of their bayonets. One or two of the more venturesome, when the soldiers formed up, endeavoured to stab them with their large broad-bladed assegais, but got stabbed themselves. One warrior got stabbed in the throat and another through the stomach. Both died immediately. The best and safest method, we discovered, was for one of us to engage the soldier. Whilst he was intent on defending himself, another would creep up behind him and plunge in the assegai. Eventually we killed every one of them. Not one escaped.

But not all the men of the 24th died where they stood; Captain Younghusband's company on the extreme left succeeded in retreating to the foot of Isandhlwana Mount. The Zulus rolled up the other companies, and in a few minutes they were slaughtered to a man. The song "The Noble 24th" recalls the great deeds of the men of the 1st and 2nd Battalions.

A story came one morning
From a far and distant land,
That savages had massacred
A small but gallant band;
'Gainst twenty thousand savage foes,
'Midst thunder, shot and shell,
Five hundred valiant English fought,
And nobly fighting fell.
Five hundred British soldiers stood
And nobly fighting fell.

The unknown story of the last stand of the six hundred (the number recorded in the official casualty list) British redcoats at Isandhlwana would make an epic far more glorious than that of the Thin Red Line of Balaklava, to which the Russian cavalry never got closer than 150 yards. But none of them lived to tell it. The nearest we can get to the truth is the statement of a Zulu induna who told an Englishman: "Much astonishment was expressed by the Zulus at the behaviour of your soldiers—firstly, regarding their death-dealing powers considering their numbers, and secondly, because they did not run away before the enormous numerical superiority of our army."

In a whirlwind of thousands of savage warriors, their black bodies glistening with sweat, their flashing assegais stabbing in all directions, the British line was overwhelmed. From then onwards the scene was one of mad confusion, as the victorious Zulus rushed the tents and wagons.

Lieutenant Smith-Dorrien, galloping back in a vain attempt to organise the ammunition supply, met a colonial wagon conductor who shouted, "The game is up. If I had a good horse, I would ride straight for Pietermaritzburg." Smith-Dorrien never saw him again. In a depression in the ground, he came upon Surgeon Maj. Peter Shepperd treating the wounded. He never saw him again either.

Fifty miles away in Pietermaritzburg, Sir Bartle Frere was being told by a caller—a singular coincidence, he thought, when he heard of the disaster at Isandhlwana—that the Zulu people would bring their tyrant to reason, and that after a single action, or at most two, the Zulu military system would collapse.

Up the gentle slope towards Isandhlwana Mount surged a mob of terrified natives, noncombatants, mixed with an occasional white survivor, encircled and engulfed in a wave of stabbing, shrieking Zulus, all racing to the imagined safety of the rear, the rapidly narrowing gap over the neck leading to the road back. Hacking and stabbing, the Zulus closed into the struggling mass, leaving the dead "strung out in a long string with knots in it," as one visitor to the scene of carnage later described it. The string was formed of single corpses, the knots clusters of dead where little groups had gathered to make a hopeless, gallant stand.

No coherent story can be told of the last minutes of the stricken camp. Only incidents emerge from the general confusion. Many fugitives were caught amongst the tents and wagons; others fled towards the road, some throwing away their guns, others firing as they ran. "Everyone bolted; I bolted too," honestly admitted Wally Erskine; but another survivor remembers distinctly that Erskine did his best to rally his men first. "Bullets were flying all over the place, but I never seemed to notice them," says Lieutenant Smith-Dorrien. Nearly all the Zulus seemed to have firearms and plenty of ammunition. "Before we knew where we were, they came right into the camp and assegaied everyone right and left," he describes. Everyone who had a horse turned to fly. The Zulus were now masters of the field. The ordered battle was over. All coherence was gone. The lines melted into groups, or into files, as friend and foe mingled in one surging, stabbing crowd. The Zulus rushed over the camp like a vast array of black ants.

The ever-present Mehlokazulu describes one valiant soldier: "He was a very tall man, and as we were rushing over the camp, he jumped on to an empty wagon with a gun and kept firing away, first on one side and then on another, so that no one got near him. We all saw him and watched him, for he was high up on the wagon, and we all said what a brave man that was. All those who tried to stab him were knocked over at once or bayoneted. He kept his ground for a very long time. Then someone shot him."

A soldier of the Umcityu Regiment reports: "As we rushed on, the soldiers retired on the camp, fighting all the way, and as they got into the camp we were intermingled with them. One party of soldiers came out from among the tents and formed up a little above the ammunition wagons. They held their ground there until their ammunition failed them, when they were nearly all assegaied."

Trooper George Sparks of the Natal Mounted Police had a narrow escape, but his friend Pearce turned back, fatally for himself. Sparks came across Pearce. "Things look black," he said. "My oath, they do," replied Pearce, who rushed into his tent to fetch a bit for his horse. Looking back, Sparks saw the fugitives coming up the slope, the Zulus in close pursuit, shouting, "Stab the white pigs, stab the pigs." He cried urgently to Pearce, "Come on man, let's ride off. We shall be killed." Pearce emerged from his tent, the bit in his hand. "What a choking off I'll get if the Sergeant-Major sees me riding with a snaffle instead of the regulation bit," he announced. He turned back into the tent, and that was the last Sparks saw of him. Bandsman Bickley was more fortunate. His quartermaster asked him to saddle his horse while he went to the latrine. As he didn't come back, Bickley mounted the horse and galloped off. At the height of the carnage in the camp, Lieutenant Coghill rode up and ordered Colonel Glyn's orderly and cook to strike his tent and put it on a wagon. The orderly, Williams, was one of the survivors; the cook, Hough, died.

Several other stories of isolated incidents on that memorable day have survived. A determined stand was made behind the officers' tents by some men of the 24th. Months later the body of Colour Sergeant Wolf of the 1st Battalion was found, surrounded by the corpses of twenty of his men. Farther up the hill, another sixty men were found grouped round the bodies of Captain Wardell and Lieutenant Dyer. Mr. Brickhill recalled seeing Quartermaster Pullen, his tent companion, rallying the fragments of his battalion to face a final Zulu rush. "Come on, men, rally here, follow me," he shouted above the din. "Don't be running away like a parcel of old women." Quartermaster Bloomfield, who had tried to stop Smith-Dorrien from looting his battalion's ammunition boxes, met his death struggling to free ammunition boxes from stampeding mules, who were plunging and kicking, maddened with fear. A Zulu came up from behind and plunged an assegai between his shoulder blades. Many men fought singly or in groups hand to hand with the Zulus amongst the tents; others dived under wagons, firing to the last as they were dragged out and assegaied. The Union Jack flying over Colonel Pulleine's tent was pulled down and torn to pieces.

One of the two last "great stands" was made by the men of Captain Younghusband's company on a rocky ledge on the precipitous slope of Isandhlwana Mount. With their backs to the rock they sold their lives dearly in the face of odds of hundreds to one. Months later sixty British bodies were found with the corpse of their gallant captain; 100 yards away, the bodies of Lieutenant Pope and his company, who were overpowered and slaughtered where they stood. A Zulu induna recalls fighting with two officers with "pieces of glass in their eyes"—probably Lieutenants Pope and Goodwin-Austen. He shot them both, but only after he himself had been hit in the neck, left side and leg by bullets from their revolvers. A soldier of the Uve Regiment says that after the soldiers and remaining Europeans had fought some time, "at length the Zulus managed to divide them into two bodies, one of which retired slowly, and always fighting, up the slopes of Isandhlwana.

Gradually the English on the koppie got fewer and fewer, though still fighting obstinately, till the Zulus at length, becoming weary, resolved to make an end of them; fresh companies were ordered up from the right horn till finally, but few being left, and when in the act of reloading their guns, the Zulus rushed in and, stabbing with their assegais, killed them to the last man." This Zulu soldier says that the last man climbed up the rocks and held his own in a small cave until far into the afternoon, and "the shadows were long on the hills before he met his fate."

Mr. Brickhill describes the camp's last moments:

Simultaneously with this, the only bodies of soldiers still visible rose from firing their last shot and joined me in the general flight. Panic was everywhere and no officer to guide, no shelter to fall back upon. The only attempt at a stand that I know of was made by the few that followed Quartermaster Pullen and the Basutos, who had a narrow escape of being cut off at the crest, but who came through past the General's tent, shouting to each other and keeping up their fire from a few rocks under Isandhlwana. The Zulus for the last three hundred yards did not fire twenty-five shots, but came on with the steady determination of *walking down* the camp by force of numbers. I consider that they were thirty to one of us. At a hundred and twenty yards' distance, they raised the shout, "Usutu."* They now came on with an overwhelming rush.

Men, horses, oxen were running everywhere, says Brickhill.

A mass of fugitives was now struggling to reach the neck between the Mount and Stoney Hill, the only outlet to the road to Rorke's Drift, before the Zulu right horn closed in. Standing

---

* The name of Cetewayo's faction in the fraternal strife of 1856.

on a hill eight miles away, the Reverend de Witt, a Dutch
missionary who lived near Rorke's Drift, watched through his
field glasses the Zulus rushing up the slopes of the western face
of the Mount. Into the narrow neck, congested with panic-
stricken transport drivers, jostling each other with their teams
and wagons, shouting and yelling at their oxen, rushed the
survivors of the camp. Many of them were too late; only a few
got through the narrowing gap as the Zulus raced up. Smith-
Dorrien describes the scene of confusion:

> I jumped on my broken-kneed pony, which had had no
> rest for thirty hours, and followed the wagons to find,
> on topping the neck, a scene of confusion I shall never
> forget, for some four thousand Zulus had come in behind
> and were busy with shield and assegai. Into this mass I
> rode, revolver in hand, right through the Zulus, but they
> completely ignored me. I heard afterwards that they had
> been told by their King Cetewayo that black-coats were
> civilians and were not worth killing. I had a blue patrol
> jacket on, and it is noticeable that the only five British
> officers who escaped—Essex, Cockrane, Gardner, Curling
> and myself—had blue coats. The Zulus throughout my
> escape seemed to be set on killing natives who had sided
> with us, either as fighting levies or transport drivers.

Mr. Brickhill rode up to the neck at much the same time:

> I joined the fugitives retreating over the neck, on reaching
> which I found all communication by the road we had
> come along cut off by several lines of Zulus running
> across. They had come along behind Isandhlwana and
> thus intercepted our retreat. The Zulus left horn had
> now come over the ridge south of Stoney Hill. They
> could have completed the circle, but preferred, I think,
> leaving this gap, so that they might attack us in our flight
> and bring us to bay. The right horn edged away more

and more to the left and both kept up a constant cross fire upon us.

At about the time Brickhill and Smith-Dorrien made their escape, Lieutenants Coghill and Melville of the 24th came galloping over the neck, carrying the regimental colours, and began a dash for the river.

The road to Rorke's Drift was now closed. The fugitives turned away, running and galloping over the rough ground to the left, making for the nearest point of the river.

The story of the final stage of the battle of Isandhlwana belongs to Colonel Durnford, who, if partly responsible for the disaster, was one of its greatest heroes. Durnford, with his Basutos and a small force of Natal Mounted Police and Colonial Volunteers, had retreated firing from the donga to a position on the slopes of Stoney Hill leading up to the neck. There they were attacked by the Umcityu and Uve Regiments, seeking to close the escape route from the camp. When Brickhill passed on the road above, they were hemmed in by Zulus; formed in a rough square, their ammunition gone, holding the enemy at bay with sword and bayonet, they yielded ground step by step. Mehlokazulu was in at the kill: "When we closed in we came on a mixed party of mounted and infantry-men, who had evidently been stopped by the end of our horn; they numbered about a hundred. They made a desperate resistance, some firing with pistols and others using swords. I repeatedly heard the word 'Fire' given by someone, but we proved too many for them, and killed them all where they stood. When all was over I had a look at these men, and saw an officer with his arm in a sling and with a big moustache [Colonel Durnford] surrounded by Carabineers, soldiers and other men that I did not know." A warrior of the Umcityu Regiment says: "They were completely surrounded on all sides, and stood back to back, and surrounding some men who were in the centre. Their ammunition was now done, except that they had some revolvers which they fired at us at close quarters. We were quite unable to break their square until we had killed a great many of them by throwing our assegais at short distances. We eventually overcame them in this way."

Captain Shepstone was killed in a vain attempt to rejoin Durnford. "I must go and see where my chief is," he shouted to a comrade. Colonel Durnford was heard by a mounted policeman to cry, "Now my men, let's see what we can do." He was last seen by Captain Nourse still encouraging the few men with him. Durnford's last stand became a legend amongst the Zulus, who admired bravery. They called him the "Lion," a title of praise hitherto accorded only to the great Shaka.

Durnford's final stand had held the Zulu left horn in check, leaving a tiny gap through which the last fugitives escaped. "Everyone was now blocked in," says Mehlokazulu. The sound of firing died away, the cloud of white smoke that, together with the eclipse, had drawn a dark pall over the scene of death, drifted slowly away.

By 1:30 P.M. no white man was alive at Isandhlwana camp. In thirty minutes its gallant defenders had been killed or put to flight. The last survivor is believed to have been a drummer boy of the 24th who was seen flinging his short sword at a Zulu, who killed him with his assegai. All resistance is believed to have been over by 2 P.M.

Captain Lonsdale, who was accompanying Lord Chelmsford's force, decided about noon to ride back to camp to organise rations for his men, who had been without food for twenty-four hours. He was very tired and he rode along dreaming, paying little attention to his surroundings. Suddenly, as he neared the tents, he was roused from his reverie by the whistle of a bullet. Looking up in amazement, he saw men in red tunics moving about amongst the tents. Some silly native must have let off a shot by accident, thought Lonsdale, as he urged his pony Dot forward amongst the tents. Then he noticed that the men in red coats had black faces. Still the awful truth didn't dawn on Lonsdale until a Zulu native emerged from a tent and threw an assegai at him. Then and only then did he realise that the camp had been taken. Turning his horse in an instant, he galloped for his life amidst a hail of bullets, with one thought in his mind—to warn the General before the whole force marched into the trap.

9

PURSUIT

THE FUGITIVES streamed over the neck, making for the nearest point of the Buffalo River, five miles away. Behind them came a horde of Zulus. No white man on foot succeeded in reaching the river and only a few horsemen, for over the rough ground, strewn with rocks, scored with chasms, seamed with water courses, here dry and stony, with steep sides, there wet and boggy, the athletic Zulus could run as fast as most horses. They caught and put to the assegai many of the fugitives; of those who got to the river, many were carried away and drowned in the swift-flowing stream, eighty yards wide; others were stabbed in the water by the relentless Zulus. Some hundreds of natives and twenty-five white men succeeded in getting across to the comparative safety of the Natal bank; but the Zulus did not give up, and killed several of the fleeing men in sight of safety.

Maj. Stuart Smith and Lieutenant Curling got their guns, each limber covered with clinging men, over the neck, where, finding the road to Rorke's Drift already cut off, they turned away to the left, behind a crowd of natives and camp followers who were running down a ravine. The guns got stuck in a deep water-course, and in a moment the Zulus were amongst them, pulling the men off and stabbing them as they tried to run. The two officers and a sergeant got away, although Major Smith was severely wounded in the arm. Riding towards the river, they met Lieutenant Coghill, who suggested they try to rally the fugitives and make a stand. Smith said he didn't think it was possible, and they all rode on together.

Captain Essex, with an infinite capacity for survival but little capability for describing his many escapes from the jaws of death, reached the river and swam across, reporting only that the ground between the camp and the Buffalo was "impractical for horsemen and many fell or were swept away in the stream." Struggling up the Natal bank, he took command of the fugitives and led them to Helpmakaar, ten miles away.

Trooper Sparks of the Natal Mounted Police, riding over the neck, found himself irresistibly borne along by a crowd of mounted Basutos, some of Durnford's men. He had only a vague idea of how he came to find himself shortly thereafter on the brink of a miniature precipice overlooking the river. The Zulus, he saw, were close behind. Dismounting, he led his horse down the bank to a narrow ledge, where he remounted. A shot whistled by his head, and turning round he saw a number of Zulus above him, about to leap down. Putting spurs to his horse, he plunged into the swirling torrent, disappearing below the surface but re-emerging still astride his horse. All around him were dozens of men, white and black, holding each other with death grips, sinking and reappearing in the racing torrent until they were swept out of his sight. A few strong swimmers succeeded in avoiding their drowning comrades, only to fall victim to the Zulu spears thrown from the top of the bank. None of the assegais fell near Sparks, but, suddenly, his horse turned over and left him struggling in midstream, his clothes and boots waterlogged. Reaching the farther side, he managed to grasp some reeds and pull himself up the bank, where he found his friend, trooper Kincaid, sitting down, calmly emptying the water from his boots. Sparks pointed to the Zulus swimming over in pursuit. He and Kincaid went in search of riderless horses, succeeded in capturing two and rode to Helpmakaar, from where, next day, Sparks was sent to carry Lord Chelmsford's despatch to Pietermaritzburg. Both Sparks and Kincaid lived until 1935.

Lieutenant Davis of the Natal Native Contingent found himself riding with Lieutenant Henderson of the same force. "What do we do? Our only chance of life appears to make a bolt of it," he said to Henderson, who agreed. Putting spurs to their horses, they galloped to the river. On the way a huge Zulu jumped in front of Davis, seizing his horse's bridle. Davis lunged at the Zulu with his carbine, to the barrel of which was attached a "Bowie" knife. The native grabbed the gun and wrenched it from Davis' grasp, causing the horse to rear. This almost unseated Davis, but shook off the Zulu, who missed when he threw his assegai. Galloping on, Davis had another narrow escape. Confronted by a Zulu brandishing a broad-bladed assegai, Davis shot him with his revolver; but, before he fell, the Zulu hurled his assegai, wounding the horse. Leaning over the horse's withers, Davis galloped madly for the river, the air full of assegais. His mount tripped and stumbled over a boulder, throwing him to the ground. He managed to vault back into the saddle and continued his flight. On reaching the bank, he looked down on a sight he never forgot, swirling waters filled with fugitives, the terror-stricken horses striking down the swimmers. Jumping his horse into the water, Davis threw himself from the saddle and, seizing the stirrup, was towed to safety.

Lieutenant Erskine stopped to catch his breath while running for the river. Sitting on a rock, he saw a number of Zulus chasing and stabbing a group of soldiers. Realising his danger, he ran, in his haste leaving his gun on the rock, and met Captain Stafford riding one horse and leading another, on to which Erskine jumped. Galloping on, he recognised Colonel Durnford's horse, running riderless with the saddle hanging loose. Twenty Zulus were close behind him when he reached the river bank. "The thought came to me," he says, "rather risk my neck over the precipice than face the Zulus, so I shut my eyes and spurred my horse forward." In the middle of the stream four or five men caught hold of his horse's tail; he couldn't move. Then a number of Zulus swam up and assegaied them. Miraculously freed, Erskine got to the Natal side, where he found a company of natives drawn up and firing at the pursuing Zulus. "While watching this little skirmish," he says, "I saw one of our Kaffirs brought to bay by a Zulu. After some preliminary guarding on the part of both men, the Zulu stabbed our Kaffir in the shoulder, whereupon he leaped into the air and stuck his assegai into the Zulu's heart. They rolled together into the river and I saw no more of either." Erskine reached Helpmakaar at 6:30 P.M.

The fate of Surgeon Maj. Peter Shepperd, whom Smith-Dorrien had seen attending the wounded in the camp just as the Zulus rushed in, is described by a Natal Carabineer.

As we were riding for our lives and the Zulus pursuing us, a trooper named Kelly staggered in his saddle, evidently hit by an assegai. I stopped my horse to see what was the matter, and tried to support him but I couldn't, and had to lift him off on to the ground. At that moment Dr. Shepperd came galloping past. I called out to him and he dismounted to examine poor Kelly. After carefully examining him, he said, "Poor fellow, too late, too late." I had just mounted my horse and Dr. Shepperd was in the act of putting his foot in his stirrup when he was struck fatally by an assegai.

"Our flight I shall never forget," says Mr. Brickhill, who seems to have been everywhere like the fortunate Captain Essex, and just as lucky. There was no path, no track, boulders all about, as he spurred down the road from the neck.

On we were borne, now into some dry torrent bed, now wending our way amongst trees of stunted growth, so that, unless you made the best use of your eyes, you were in constant danger of colliding with some tree, or finding yourself unhorsed at the bottom of a ravine. Our way was strewn with shields, assegais, blankets, hats, clothing of all descriptions, guns, ammunition belts and saddles, which horses had managed to kick off, revolvers and belts and I know not what else. Our stampede was composed of mules, with and without pack saddles, oxen and horses in all stages of equipment, and flying men, all strangely inter-mingled, man and beast, all apparently impressed with the danger which surrounded us. One riderless horse that came up alongside of me I caught and handed to a poor soldier who was struggling along on foot. But he had scarcely mounted before he was knocked off by a Zulu bullet.

Brickhill learned that he had to steel his heart against pity. He came up with poor Band Sergeant Gamble, tottering and tumbling about amongst the stones. "For God's sake, give me a lift," he said. Brickhill replied, "My dear fellow, it's a case of life and death with me." "Closing my eyes," he says, "I put spurs to my horse and bounded ahead and that was the last I saw of him. The next I came up with, also a soldier, said, 'Well, I'm pumped. I'm done. The Zulus can just come and stab me if they like,' and quietly sat down on a stone to await his death."

When he reached the Buffalo, Brickhill saw it was rolling

high. There was no time to select a place to cross. Running lines
of Zulus were making for the calmer waters higher up. His
horse plunged in, swimming at once, but it had scarcely gone
six yards before it stumbled over something large in the rushing
water and nearly fell. Brickhill clutched its mane and guided it
to a pool below a waterfall, in which three riderless horses were
swimming round and round. Away to his right he saw Lieutenant Melville and Mr. Foley, a wagon conductor, plunging into
the river. That was the last Brickhill saw of Melville until thirteen days later, when he helped to find and bury his body with
that of Lieutenant Coghill.

Somewhere about this time there occurred an incident
which led to the award of the Victoria Cross to Pvt. Samuel
Wassal of the 80th Regiment for his gallant conduct, at the
immediate risk of his own life, in saving that of Private West-
wood of the same regiment. Riding down the bank, closely
pursued by Zulus, Wassal saw his friend struggling in the river
and apparently drowning. He dismounted and, seizing West-
wood, dragged him across under a hail of bullets.

Of the survivors of the battle, only Lt. Walter Higgins saw
the end of Melville and Coghill, who were trying to rescue the
colours of the 2nd Battalion, the flag that Colonel Glyn had left
behind in camp that morning. Riding to the river bank, Higgins
met the two officers and heard them agree to stand by each
other if they were attacked. All three plunged their horses into
the river, which was filled with struggling men, the Zulus swimming amongst them, stabbing and killing. Higgins' horse swam
to a big rock in the middle of the stream, where it turned over,
throwing Higgins under. Dropping his rifle and ammunition, he
surfaced, his eyes blinded by water. A black boy seized and
mounted his horse. Higgins called for someone to stop him, but
no one heard above the din. Melville, holding the colours, but no

longer on his horse, swam towards Higgins, but the force of the current swept Melville away. Coghill, who had reached the other bank, turned back, when Melville called to him, to plunge in to his rescue. But Higgins swam over, and then all three dragged themselves into the shallows, just ahead of the Zulus. "Here they come," shouted Coghill. "For God's sake use your revolvers," Higgins shouted back. "I'm done. I can't go any further," he heard Melville cry. Coghill said the same. Leaving them to their fate, the exhausted Higgins dragged himself up the bank, where he found Smith-Dorrien lying on his back, unconcernedly draining the water from his boots.

Smith-Dorrien described his miraculous escape in a letter he wrote the next day to his old father in England. Seeing that the camp was completely surrounded and the road to Rorke's Drift was cut off, he followed the line of fugitives, "Everybody," he says, "went pell-mell over ground covered with huge boulders and rocks until we got to a deep spruit or gully. How the horses got over I have no idea. I was riding a broken-kneed old crock which did not belong to me, and which I expected to go on its head every minute. We had to go bang through them at the spruit. Lots of our men were killed there."

He had many marvellous escapes, he told his father, while firing at the pursuing Zulus as he galloped along. The ground towards the road, he says, was so broken that the Zulus ran as fast as the horses and "kept killing all the way." He saw very few white fugitives, most of those he encountered being mounted blacks.

Coming to the river, Smith-Dorrien dismounted and led his horse down the steep precipice. At the bottom of the bank he came on a British soldier, bleeding from a wound in his arm. Smith-Dorrien stopped to bind it up with his handkerchief. Just as he finished, Major Smith of the artillery rode down the bank, wounded and white as a sheet, bleeding profusely. "For God's sake, man, get on, the Zulus are on top of us," he called. Smith-Dorrien was about to spur his horse into the river when it was struck by an assegai, and in a second the Zulus were pouring down the bank, finishing off the wounded, the man he had helped and Major Smith. Smith-Dorrien continues his story:

> However, with the strong hope that everybody clings to that some accident would turn up, I rushed off on foot and plunged into the river, which was little better than a roaring torrent. I was being carried down the stream at a tremendous pace, when a loose horse came by me and I got hold of his tail and he landed me safely on the other bank; but I was too tired to stick to him and get on his back. I got up again and rushed on and was several times knocked over by our mounted niggers, who would not get out of my way, then up a tremendous hill, with my wet clothes and boots full of water. About 20 Zulus got over the water and followed us up the hill, but, I am thankful to say, they had not their firearms. Crossing the river, however, the Zulus on the opposite side kept firing at us as we went up the hill and killed several of the niggers round me. I was the only white man to be seen until I came to one who had been kicked by his horse and could not mount. I put him on his horse and lent him my knife. He said he would catch me a horse. Directly he was up he went clean away. A few Zulus followed us for about three miles across the river, but they had no guns, and I had a revolver, which I kept letting them know. Also the mounted niggers stopped a little and kept firing at them. They did not come in close and finally stopped altogether.

Smith-Dorrien struggled into Helpmakaar at sundown, dead beat. He had been on the move since dawn, when he had begun his ride to carry the message to Colonel Durnford.

About the time the last survivor had crossed the Buffalo

River, the eclipse of the sun ended. Twenty-five white men had succeeded in crossing the river at Fugitives' Drift, as it is still named. The exact number of natives who crossed was uncertain, since many of them ran straight to their homes in Natal. Officially 346 is the total number of men believed to have crossed the river. The white survivors, apart from those whose stories have already been given, included six privates of the gallant 24th: Johnson and Dillon (bandsmen); Williams (Colonel Glyn's orderly); and Trainer, Rickley and Grant (attached to Colonel Durnford's rocket battery). The surviving officers were Captains Alan Gardner and Barton (of Durnford's native contingent); and Lieutenants Curling (Royal Artillery), Cockrane (Durnford's staff officer), and Raw (Durnford's Basutos). Other survivors were Henderson (a police officer in Durnford's force), Sergeant Gamble, Mr. Foley, and Hamer (a commissariat officer). The bodies of Lieutenant Melville and Coghill were found in the river on February 4. Melville's watch had stopped at ten minutes past two. Their gallant attempt to save the colours earned them the posthumous award of the Victoria Cross on January 15, 1907. According to the official casualty list, 52 officers, 806 British and colonials, and 471 natives had died in the camp or on the escape route.

The camp at Isandhlwana was given over to an orgy of looting and savagery. The frenzied Zulus slashed open their victims' stomachs, a practice dictated by their belief that, unless they did so, their own stomachs would swell up and burst. Tents and wagons were ransacked, chiefly for food and drink; for few of the Zulus had eaten that day, having brought little food with them in a year of drought and scarcity. They ate and drank everything they could lay hands on, including the medical supplies in the hospital tent, which poisoned some and gave others horrible pains. Some of the oxen were killed, cut up and eaten raw. The Zulu loot included 800 modern rifles and 400,000 rounds of ammunition. The two cannon were dragged to Cetewayo's kraal, where they were found intact at the end of the war; the Zulus did not know how to fire them.

In the late afternoon the victorious warriors streamed back over the Ngutu Hills, exhausted after five days of marching and an hour's fight. For three days they stayed in the vicinity of the camp, removing their dead in wagons and burying the bodies in dongas and crevasses. Estimates of their losses vary considerably, but it is believed that at least 3,000 Zulus were killed and thousands more seriously wounded. The regiments that had fought had had enough. Dispirited by their losses, they dispersed to their kraals. Cornelius Vijn, a young Dutch trader in Cetewayo's capital, records that the wailing and crying for the dead went on for a fortnight.

After the war was over, Mr. John Shepstone, brother of Sir Theophilus, talked with several chiefs.

The first remark of one was, "We fought for our king and you beat us." I replied: "How can you say that when you took the camp at Isandhlwana?" They said that, though they had carried everything before them at Isandhlwana, they were fully convinced on that day that they were no match for the white man. I asked how, and they replied: "You know what we are, when once we give way and run. There is no stopping us to fight with the pursuer. But your people when, as in several instances, only numbering three, would stand back-to-back and defy us to approach. While the ammunition lasted, we did not attack; but took advantage of them when their powder failed. We allowed none to escape." "You gave us the battle that day," they explained, "for you dispersed your army in small parties all over the country. We had therefore no difficulty in overwhelming each party as we came upon it, putting all to the assegai and passing on."

The regiments that had fought at Isandhlwana marched back to their kraals. Only the Undi Corps remained behind. It had been held in reserve and its men had not fought at Isandhlwana. Dabulamanzi, the Zulu general, despite the orders he had received from his brother the king, that under no circumstances were the Zulus to invade Natal, hearkened to the warriors' clamour and agreed to lead them on an attack on the British base at Rorke's Drift.

10

THE STRICKEN

CAMP

Tʜᴇ ᴄᴀᴍᴘ had been taken and its garrison massacred without Lord Chelmsford's knowing anything about it; but he had received several hints that something sinister was happening at Isandhlwana, twelve miles to his north. He reached the site of the new camp in the Amangene Gorge, about 12:30 P.M. With him were Colonel Glyn and four companies of the 24th commanded by Colonel Degacher. Colonel Harness with his four guns and an escort of two companies of the 24th under Captains Church and Harvey were moving slowly towards the gorge.

About 1:15 P.M. Lord Chelmsford was told by his interpreter, Mr. Longeast, that interrogation of a Zulu prisoner had revealed the startling information that an immense impi, estimated from the regiments composing it to number from 20,000 to 25,000 men, was expected that day from Ulundi. Norris Newman takes up the story:

At this juncture one of our mounted natives came gal-loping down from the opposite ridge, whence the camp could be seen, and reported to a staff officer that an attack was being made on the camp, as he had seen heavy firing and heard the big guns. On this being reported to Lord Chelmsford, he at once galloped up to the crest of the hill, accompanied by his staff, and on arrival every field-glass was levelled at the camp. The sun was shining brightly on the white tents, which were plainly visible, but all seemed quiet. No signs of firing, nor of an engage-ment could be seen, and although bodies of men moving about could be distinguished, yet they were not un-naturally supposed to be our own troops.

The men seen by Newman were the victorious Zulus; the battle at the front of the camp was over, the firing ended.

Still Chelmsford did not move.

Approaching Isandhlwana, Commander Browne, who had been sent back towards the camp with his native contingent three hours before, learned from a Zulu prisoner that an at-tack on the camp was planned, and he pushed ahead with the intention of reinforcing its defenders. First, Mr. Mansell, of the Natal Mounted Police, was sent ahead to reconnoitre. He reported as follows:

We came to a rising ground from which we could see the camp. I should say we were then about six miles distant from it. Of course all the men were eager, having heard the rumours, and eagerly looked out for the camp. There certainly were some tents standing, but they seemed very few, and away to the left front of the camp there was some smoke, though not much, and it was high up, just as if there had been musketry fire, and the smoke had floated away; but there was certainly no musketry fire going on then. A few seconds afterward a sergeant

[110]

of the police said, "There go the guns, sir." I could see the smoke, but we could hear nothing. In a few seconds we distinctly saw the guns fired again, one after the other, sharp. This was done several times. A pause, and then a flash-flash. The sun was shining on the camp at the time, and then the camp looked dark, just as if a shadow was passing over it. The guns did not fire after that, and in a few minutes all the tents had disappeared. The sergeant said, "It's all over now, sir." I said, "Yes, and I hope it is the right way." We could see there was fighting going on, but of course did not know which way it had gone. The men all thought the Zulus had retired; but I felt doubtful in my own mind, but had no idea really of the catastrophe that had taken place.

When Mansell reported to Commander Browne, Captain Develin was sent to carry the news to Lord Chelmsford. Galloping back, Develin met Colonel Harness, whom he found in conversation with Major Gossett, Lord Chelmsford's A.D.C. "The camp is surrounded, and will be taken unless helped at once," Develin breathlessly announced. Captain Church reported that "almost immediately we heard the sound of cannon towards the camp, eight miles off, and saw shells bursting amongst the hills to the left of it." Harness said he would march towards the camp, but Gossett ridiculed the idea.

Major Gossett said he rode back to give Chelmsford the message from Commander Browne, but both Lord Chelmsford and his Military Secretary, Colonel Crealock, afterwards denied receiving any message that the camp was threatened. Chelmsford sent an order to Colonel Harness to continue his march towards the new camp, and he instructed Colonel Glyn to bivouac for the night in the Amangene Gorge. About 2 P.M. he himself set out for Isandhlwana, escorted by eighty mounted Volunteers under the command of Colonel Russell. He caught up with Commander Browne's contingent about 2:30 P.M., and was told that there was a large force of Zulus between him and the camp. At 3:15 P.M., Colonel Crealock records, "The General appeared to think he would be able to brush through any parties of Zulus that might be in his road to the camp without any force further than the 1st. Battalion Native Contingent [Browne's] and the 80 mounted men escorting him."

Fifteen minutes later, when the party was still four miles from Isandhlwana, a solitary horseman was seen approaching. Riding ahead to intercept him, Colonel Crealock recognised Captain Lonsdale, who called out to him, "The Zulus have the camp." "How do you know?" asked the incredulous Crealock. "Because I have been in it," came the reply. Norris Newman was riding near Lord Chelmsford when he was told the dreadful news. "I shall never forget the scene," the war correspondent states. "The looks of amazement, grief and horror" on the faces of everyone. "But I left a thousand men to guard the camp," was all the General could say. "Glyn must return at once," he ordered. Major Gossett was despatched to bring up the men left in the Amangene Gorge, while Lord Chelmsford's force advanced slowly, sending forward a reconnaissance, which reported that the camp was swarming with Zulus carrying off their plunder. Sergeant Major Scott stated that firing was still going on at the neck.

Major Gossett, hurrying back to bring up Glyn's men, says that as he approached the gorge, "not wishing to alarm them, I slackened my pace as I rode up and said 'You are to march back to the camp.' 'Hoorah,' cried some of the men, little knowing the reason for the change of orders. I sat on a rock and told Glyn and Staff Captain Hallam Parr what had happened. They were incredulous, but I felt I could not sup-

[112]

port their doubts and told them so. In a short time the force was under way. Ill news travels apace and the men knew that a disaster had occurred, and tired as they were they marched at a grand pace." "We marched as hard as our legs could carry us," records one of the party, who adds, "It would be impossible to describe the anxiety felt by all ranks; how eyes were strained towards the camp, how long those thirteen miles seemed, although the men marched splendidly, racing over the ground."

Although they had already marched fourteen miles that day, the men of the 24th Regiment 1st Battalion reached Lord Chelmsford's halting place by 6:10 P.M., covering a distance of nine miles in two hours.

"We halted and awaited the arrival of Colonel Glyn's men with unspeakable impatience and anxiety," writes Norris Newman. Mounted patrols sent up the ridges to report came back with the news that the Zulus were burning the tents and taking away the wagons. "All of which served only to increase our maddening impatience and anxiety," he recalls. One patrol reported that all firing had ceased and that the Zulus were in possession of the road to Natal. Newman consoled himself with the hope that the camp's troops had merely been driven back to Rorke's Drift. Trooper Symons, up on a ridge with Major Dartnell, watched the Zulus driving off the cattle and the tents disappearing. "I cannot describe my feelings," he says. Large masses of Zulus were seen retiring from the camp across the Ngutu Hills.

When his and Colonel Glyn's forces were combined, the General briefly addressed the troops, telling them, "Whilst we were skirmishing in front, the Zulus have taken our camp. There are ten thousand Zulus in our rear, and twenty thousand in our front; we must win back our camp tonight, and cut

[113]

our way back to Rorke's Drift tomorrow." The men answered with a cheer, "All right, sir; we'll do it."

When he finished speaking Lord Chelmsford ordered the troops to advance in battle order. The mounted men were sent to the front; the guns were kept in the centre, following the rough track, with a half-battalion of the 24th on either side of them; the two native battalions were placed on the outer flanks. In this formation the troops moved cautiously forward on the camp.

"The sun was just sinking behind the hills when the word 'Forward' was given," recalls Symons. "The orders were," he says, "to retake the camp at all hazards. There was to be no retreat."

Norris Newman says the troops advanced "with fear in [their] hearts as to the events that might have taken place, but nonetheless with a stern determination to recapture the position, even in the increasing darkness, and whatever might be the cost."

"In front and for miles along the heights to our right, a dense mass of black warriors were watching this little army boldly marching to the attack. Soon darkness hid us from their view," states Symons.

At 7 P.M., the soldiers were still two miles from the camp, and darkness was coming on rapidly; there was no moon, and with the declining light the difficulties of the march increased; men and horses kept falling into dongas and over rocks, and the native battalions made matters worse, despite the efforts of their officers, by crushing in on the British troops as if for protection. These men were a positive source of danger, as on the first sign of an enemy they would certainly have broken up any formation taken by the British battalion, and friend and foe would have been indistinguishable. By this time it was so dark that the mounted men were called in and formed into two bodies to the rear of the infantry.

"At this moment," says Lieutenant Milne, "an unfortunate incident occurred." Four men were seen coming from the camp. They were fired upon, and one fell. The other three ran forward, throwing their arms in the air to show they were unarmed. On being taken prisoner, they were found to be native levies who had escaped from the massacre. The wounded man was not seriously hurt.

By 7:45 P.M. the troops were within half a mile of the camp, which was in complete darkness. In the distance the black outline of the hills could be seen, on their skyline parties of Zulus moving off. Norris Newman thought he could hear the hoarse cries of the enemy and the rattle of their assegais against their shields. A halt was called, and the infantry formed lines and fixed bayonets, standing in deathlike silence. Colonel Harness was ordered to fire his guns on the neck over which the road to Rorke's Drift passed. Watching from the distance, trooper Symons thought the bright flash of the cannon and the graceful curve of the shells pretty to watch. One missile struck Isandhlwana Mount, loosening the rocks and bringing them down with a crash. But no sound came in return; no Zulu war cry, no answering shot, nothing but the rolling echoes of the guns. Cautiously the troops advanced to within 300 yards of the camp. Another halt was called and another crashing volley was fired. Again there was no answering sound. Major Black was ordered to take three companies of the 24th and occupy Stoney Hill to the left of the neck. The men moved off into the gloom. Those left behind heard Black call to his men, "No firing, but only one volley, boys, and then give them the cold steel." For ten minutes there was complete silence, then a "ringing British cheer from hundreds of throats," says Newman, announced that Black's men were on the hill. Trooper Symons, who knew nothing of Black's advance, thought the cheer came from the defenders of the camp who had held out on the hill. Some of Black's men came stumbling back to report that the camp was deserted. Lord Chelmsford ordered an advance to the neck. At the word "Forward" we marched up, says Symons, "stumbling over dead bodies."

Norris Newman describes the troops' return to the camp they had left that morning before daylight: "We began to stumble over dead bodies in every direction, and in some places, especially where the formation of the ground . . . was a ditch or anything like a shelter, the men were found lying thick and close, as though they had fought there till their ammunition was exhausted, and then been surrounded and slaughtered."

The troops bivouacked on the field of slaughter. No fires were lit; no sounds allowed, for no one knew if the Zulus might be close by, preparing to attack. Trooper Symons says that everyone was indifferent to whether the Zulus came or not. The soldiers were weary and hungry, but when some biscuits were produced they had no appetite. Everyone wanted to search the camp for friends and comrades, and bitterly resented the General's refusal to allow a search for wounded men, whose groans, says Symons, could still be heard. Next morning a wounded native was found close by the bivouac. Symons noticed a cold, unearthly smell, which he thought came from the dead, by whom the troops were surrounded. One man, says Symons, whose brother had been left in the camp lay down, "not daring to stretch out a hand, lest it should fall, perhaps, upon his dead brother's face." The terrible effect of that night's bivouac amongst the bodies of the slain was demonstrated some days later when many of the soldiers were stricken with a fever, in which one peculiarity was repeated in every case. Each man in his delirium believed that a dead man was lying beside him.

Writing his report for his London paper some days later, Norris Newman recalled the night he had spent in the camp:

But oh! how dreadful were those weary hours that followed! While all had to watch and wait, through the darkness, with what patience we could muster, for the dawn of day; with the knowledge that we were standing and lying amid and surrounded by the corpses of our late comrades—though in what fearful numbers we then but little knew. Many a vow of vengeance was breathed in the stillness of the night, and many and deep were the sobs that came from the breasts of men who, perhaps, had never sobbed before, at discovering, even by that dim light, the bodies of dear friends, brutally massacred, stripped of all clothing, disembowelled, mutilated, and in some cases decapitated. How that terrible night passed with us I fancy few would care to tell, even if they could recall it. For my own part, I felt both reckless and despairing, reckless at the almost certain prospect of an overwhelming attack by the enemy—flushed with victory—despairing, because of the melancholy scene of horror which I felt awaited us at day break. During the night we noticed fires constantly burning on all the surrounding hills, and in particular one bright blaze riveted our attention throughout, as it seemed to be near Rorke's Drift, and we feared for the safety of those left in that small place, knowing how utterly powerless we were to aid them in any way before morning.

One of his staff officers described Lord Chelmsford's unhappy state of mind that night: "A great horror and fear seemed to have taken possession of the General in place of his former cheerful incredulity, and he would allow no movement to be made as he was fully expecting to be attacked in front and most probably in the rear also." Lord Chelmsford did not know that the Zulus had retreated; his spare ammunition, all his stores, food and forage were gone. His men had only the ammunition they had taken from the camp that morning. For all he knew, the Zulus might be rushing into Natal. With his small and now ill-equipped force he could do nothing to stop them.

Norris Newman continues his story of that fearful night:

> After lying down for a while close to the General and his Staff, I arose at about an hour before daylight, for the purpose of taking a look around to see the state of matters for myself, and recognise what bodies I could. Nothing but a sense of duty could have induced me to undertake the task, or sustained me in its execution so as to go through with it. Not even on the recent battle fields of Europe, though hundreds were lying where now I saw only tens, was there ever a more sickening or heart-rending sight.
>
> The corpses of our poor soldiers, whites and natives, lay thick upon the ground in clusters, together with the dead and mutilated horses, oxen and mules, shot and stabbed in every position and manner, and the whole intermingled with the fragments of our commissariat wagons, broken and wrecked, and rifled of their contents, the debris being all scattered about, and wasted as in pure wantonness on the ground.
>
> The dead bodies of the men lay as they had fallen, but mostly with only their boots and shirts on, or perhaps a pair of trousers or a remnant of a coat, with just sufficient means of recognition to determine to which branch of the service they belonged. In many instances they lay with sixty or seventy empty cartridge cases surrounding them, thus showing they had fought to the very last, and only

succumbed and fallen, after doing their duty without flinching, when all means of resistance were exhausted. It seemed to me, at the time, that it was really wonderful that so small a force had been able to maintain such a desperate resistance for so long.

Colonel Glyn, too, ventured into the deserted camp, recognising the bodies of Colonel Pulleine, Captain Younghusband and Colonel Durnford. Dead Zulus lay in heaps everywhere. In one place he found a number of British soldiers' heads, arranged in a neat ring. A sudden burst of gunfire brought him running hurriedly back to the bivouac, where he found the native troops, scared by their own shadows, firing wildly and trying to stampede the animals. Away in the direction of Rorke's Drift, a great burst of flame shot into the sky, a portent of evil.

The troops were roused at 4:30 A.M. and ordered to march with all speed to Rorke's Drift, without waiting for daylight to reveal a sight that Lord Chelmsford thought "could not but have a demoralising effect upon the whole force." The men turned their backs on Isandhlwana with hearts filled with grief and indignation. As they marched up to the neck they left behind them a shambles—the dead, hideously mutilated, lying amidst burnt tents and overturned and derelict wagons. As they joined the road, they came upon several more wagons to whose yokes were still harnessed oxen, alive and looking as though nothing had happened. Behind them rose the steep crag of Isandhlwana, stark against the sky, resembling, even more strangely than it had four days before, the sphinx badge the men wore on their uniforms. On its rocky top perched a vulture, the first of a flock that would soon gather when the birds saw the feast spread below them.

But what fresh horror lay ahead? In the direction of

[119]

Rorke's Drift rose a column of black smoke. "Throughout the night," says trooper Symons, "firing could be heard from that direction." Were they again going to be too late? the soldiers asked themselves.

As the little column wound down the road, the first streaks of dawn revealed thousands of Zulus retreating from the direction of Rorke's Drift. "This sight served to intensify our anxiety and caused us to hurry onwards," reports Norris Newman. "We quickly reached the brow of the hill overlooking the Buffalo river and Rorke's Drift; the sight of buildings in flames at the station by no means allayed our fears. Before we quite reached the river I carefully examined the house at Rorke's Drift through my field glass, and thought I could distinguish the figures of men on parts of the wall and roof of the larger building, and one of them seemed to be waving a flag."

11

RORKE'S DRIFT

WEDNESDAY, JANUARY 22, had been a busy day at Rorke's Drift. After Colonel Durnford left for Isandhlwana with his mounted natives at 7:30 A.M., Lt. John Rouse Merriott Chard, Royal Engineers, in charge of the post—the old Swedish mission buildings about a mile from the ford—had many matters to take care of: the accommodation of the thirty-five sick and injured men, some of whom had been wounded in the attack upon Sirayo's kraal, in the missionary's dwelling and under the care of Dr. Reynolds; the checking of stores with the commissariat officer, Mr. Dalton, a one-time sergeant in a British regiment, and his assistant, L. A. Byrne; and the defence of the post by moustached and bewhiskered Lt. Gonville Bromhead, who commanded a company of the 2nd Battalion 24th Regiment, to which was attached a section from the 1st Battalion. During the morning Major Spalding came over from Helpmakaar to arrange the bringing up of another company to reinforce the small garrison at the Drift. When he left at 2 P.M. Chard rode down to the river to inspect the ponts, the floating bridge made up of barrels and planks. He was still there at 3:15 talking to Sergeant Milne of the river guard,

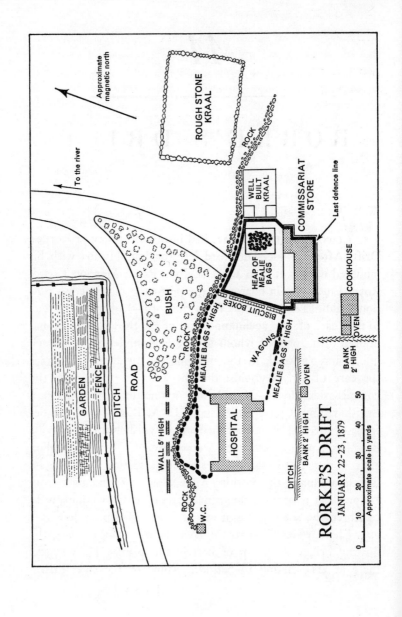

RORKE'S DRIFT
JANUARY 22-23, 1879

Approximate scale in yards
0 10 20 30 40 50

when he saw two horsemen galloping down the Zulu bank, one of whom he recognised as Adendorff, a lieutenant in the native contingent. The other was a Natal Carabineer, dressed in shirt sleeves. As the two men swam their horses across, Chard heard Adendorff shout, "They have been butchered to a man. The camp is lost." The Zulu impi, he told Chard as he mounted the Natal bank, would be upon them in two or three minutes.

At once Sergeant Milne and his six men offered to move the ponts into the middle of the stream and defend them. Chard ordered them to retire to the mission house, to which he, Adendorff and the carabineer galloped, to find everyone stunned by the news which had been brought from the camp by a native who had crossed the river higher up. The carabineer rode off to Helpmakaar to give the alarm while Chard and Bromhead conferred. Their first idea was to strike the tents, place the sick in wagons, and retire to Helpmakaar; but they were dissuaded by Dalton, who said they would all be caught on the road and slaughtered. They stood a better chance behind stone walls, he urged the two young officers. The latter, both destined to take conspicuous places in the glorious annals of the British army, quickly saw his point. There was an even more important consideration, they realised. They and their hundred men were now the only bulwark between the victorious Zulus and the 25,000 defenceless Natal colonists. The mission house, they knew, must be defended to the death.

In a moment all was energy and excitement. The officer in charge of Durnford's natives, whom he had left behind that morning, was ordered to set his 300 men working. While Bromhead was supervising the posting of his ninety-six effectives—eighty-seven men of the 24th and various details from other regiments—and the Reverend George Smith, subsequently appointed army chaplain in recognition of his services, and Dr. Reynolds were reassuring the sick and wounded men in the hospital, Chard looked after the loopholing of walls and the barricading of buildings. There were many problems to be overcome.

The mission station, consisting of two stone buildings with thatched roofs, stood on a rocky terrace just below the sugar-loafed Oscarberg Hill, by which it was commanded, and was fronted by a sunken road and an orchard, all of which could provide excellent cover for the attacking Zulus. But there was no time to set about chopping down fruit trees. In between the hospital and storeroom, formerly the mission church, lay a piece of ground, about thirty yards wide. In order for the post to present a continuous line of defence and to enable communication between the two buildings, it was vital to connect them by strong walls, back and front. Fortunately, suitable materials lay at hand. Wagons were dragged into position and a four-foot-high barricade was built with bags, each containing about 200 pounds of mealies. Meanwhile, the men of the 24th had been busy barricading the doors of the hospital with big square boxes filled with tins of meat, each weighing a hundredweight, stuffing the windows with mattresses and loopholing the walls. The hospital's interior conformed to the design of the dwelling house, being partitioned off into several tiny units connected by flimsy wooden doors. Once inside, the six soldiers set to guard the sick barricaded each outside and inside door with heavy boxes that could be moved only by several men pulling together.

The story of how a handful of Englishmen held the mission house at Rorke's Drift for twelve hours against the furious onslaughts of 4,000 Zulus glutted with victory, ranks with the

epic of Thermopylae, the heroic sea action fought by Gren-
ville in the *Revenge,* and the story of the Alamo. It is drawn
from three eyewitness accounts: Lieutenant Chard's official report, the Reverend George Smith's story, and the stirring rec-
ollections of Sgt. Henry Hook, then a twenty-eight-year-old
private in the 24th, which appeared twenty-six years later in the
Royal Magazine (February 1905).

Hook was making tea for the sick men in the hospital
when, at 4:30 P.M., he heard firing from the direction of the
river, where scouts had been posted to give the alarm. Rushing
to his loophole, he saw a great number of Zulus sweeping into
view round the base of Oscarberg Hill and come rushing at
the mission house. This, says Hook, was too much for the
Natal natives. They bolted, led by a white officer on horseback, who thus, in the Reverend Smith's words, "lived to fight
another day," and by a white sergeant. This was *too* much
for Hook and his comrades in the hospital. They fired a fu-
sillade of shots into the deserters, killing the pusillanimous sergeant. Lieutenant Chard, with great restraint, records in his
despatch merely: "About this time, Captain Stephenson's de-
tachment of the Natal Native Contingent left us, as did that
officer himself."

The garrison was thus reduced to 104 officers and men,
who now stood facing the onslaught of the Undi Corps, composed of some of Cetewayo's finest warriors.

The Reverend Smith also saw the Zulus, pouring over the
right shoulder of the hill in a dense mass and rushing at the
fort. Let him tell his story:

On they come, making straight for the connecting wall
between the storehouse and the hospital; but when they
get within fifty yards the firing is altogether too hot for
them. Some of them swerve round to their left past the

back and right end of the hospital, and then make a desperate attempt to scale the barricade in front of that building; but here too they are repulsed, and they disperse and find cover amongst the bushes and behind the stone wall below the terrace. The others have found shelter amongst numerous banks, ditches, and bushes, and behind a square Kaffir house and large brick ovens, all at the rear of our enclosure. One of the mounted chiefs was shot by Private Dunbar, 2nd battalion 24th regiment, who also killed eight of the enemy, in as many consecutive shots, as they came round the edge of the hill; and as fresh bodies of Zulus arrive they take possession of the elevated ledge of rocks overlooking our buildings and barricades at the back, and all the caves and crevices are quickly filled, and from these the enemy pour down a continuous fire upon us.

For the attack on the hospital we go over to Henry Hook. "We were pinned like rats in a hole," he says. All the doors and windows were barricaded. The six soldier guards stood by their loopholes. Nine of the invalids were unable to move, but the others helped as they were able. The Zulus came on in a wild rush. The rifles in the fort took a terrible toll, but some of the Zulus, says Hook, got within thirty yards of the walls, where they were caught between two fires, from the hospital and storehouse. Hook, who prided himself on being a marksman, was not dissatisfied with his shooting.

The first attack was beaten back after a short but desperate struggle. But the Zulus now lay concealed close to the fort, in the road and garden to its front and in the cook house to its rear. Others sniped from the rocks and crevices of the hill, keeping up a constant fire into the barricades below them.

Chard says: "Taking advantage of the bush, which we had not time to cut down, the enemy were able to advance under cover close to our wall, and in this part soon held one side of the wall, while we held the other. A series of desperate assaults were made, extending from the hospital, along the wall, as far as the bush reached: but each was most splendidly met and repulsed by our men with the bayonet, Corporal Schiess, Natal Native Contingent, greatly distinguishing himself by his conspicuous gallantry."

"All this time," adds Chard, "the enemy had been attempting to force the hospital." For what happened there we return to Hook: "Large bodies of Zulus kept hurling themselves against our slender breastworks and assaulting the hospital most fiercely."

Hook was stationed in a small room with another soldier he calls "old King Cole"—clearly a legendary character. Two men, both named Williams—Joseph and John—defended a second room, and two other men, both named Jones—Robert and William—one an old soldier, the other a young one, guarded a third room. "All this time," says Hook, "Cole kept saying he wasn't going to stay and he went outside and was shot instantly." The Reverend Smith saw his end. Cole came out of the hospital and took up position at the barricade, raising his head slowly above the parapet. A bullet, says Smith, passed clean through his head and struck the man next to him on the bridge of the nose. The news "Poor old King Cole is shot" passed round the men. The other man was not seriously hurt.

"Mr. Dalton," says Smith, "who is a tall man, was continually going along the barricades, fearlessly exposing himself, cheering the men and using his rifle effectively." Just then two Zulus charged towards the barricade. "Pot that fellow," called Dalton as he raised his rifle to shoot the other one. Smith saw his rifle drop. He turned quite pale and said he had been shot. Dr. Reynolds found that a bullet had passed through Dalton's

[127]

right shoulder. Unable to use his rifle, Dalton handed it to his assistant, Mr. Byrne, and continued to direct the fire of the men near to him.

In his hospital room, Hook kept firing from his loophole. A native patient, a man whose leg had been broken when he was shot through the thigh at Sirayo's kraal, kept calling to him, "Take my bandage off so I can move," but Hook says, "It was impossible to do anything except fight and I blazed away as hard as I could." The patients, he recalled, were groaning and crying, the Zulus swarming around and the boxes of tinned meat rattling as the bullets struck them.

Failing to take the hospital by storm, the Zulus set fire to its grass roof. "This put us in a terrible plight," records Hook. The defenders could either stay and be massacred or burnt alive or get out. All their exits were blocked, and in their charge were the helpless sick, whom they could not abandon. The dense smoke forced Hook to retire to the next room, having to leave the native patient to his awful fate. He heard the man say he wasn't afraid of the Zulus and he wanted a gun, but there was none to give him. As Hook got out, the man tried to rip off his bandages and follow, but a crowd of Zulus climbed in. "His end was merciful," Hook laconically records. Next day his charred remains were found amidst the ruins.

The garrison of the hospital fought from room to room. Hook was now alone in one room with nine patients. In another Joseph and John Williams were protecting three sick men. Outside the window from which Joseph was firing lay fourteen Zulu bodies. Somehow the Zulus dragged him out and killed him, climbing into the room and assegaiing the patients. While the Zulus were thus occupied, John Williams smashed a hole in the partition wall and got into Hook's room, telling him, "The Zulus are swarming all over the place. They've dragged Joseph Williams out and killed him."

"What are we to do now?" enquired John Williams. The room was thick with smoke, the Zulus hammering on the door. The only way of escape was the next partition wall. While Williams worked desperately at the wall with an axe, Hook guarded the door, now splintering under the Zulus' blows. Assegais kept whirling towards him. One struck the front of his helmet, tilting it back, the spear inflicting a slight wound in his scalp. Regaining his balance, Hook shot the spear thrower. Before he could reload, another Zulu seized the muzzle of his rifle. Tearing it free, Hook slipped in another cartridge and shot him at point-blank range. Each time, he says, a Zulu tried to seize his rifle, he was able to wrench it free because he had a better grip than his assailant.

All this time, records Hook, Williams had been getting the sick men through the hole he had made into the next room, all except a soldier of the 24th, a man named Conley, who had a broken leg. Watching his chance, Hook dashed to Conley and pulled him through the hole. "His leg got broken again, but there was no helping that," he states. Behind him he heard the Zulus' cries of frustration and rage as they burst into the empty room.

Now the whole process had to be repeated again. Hook defended the hole from one room, while Williams picked another hole in the next wall. When it was large enough to take Conley, who was a very heavy man, Williams dragged him and several other patients through while Hook held the Zulus back. Two invalids were lost to the Zulus, who killed trooper Hunter of the Natal Military Police and seized and dragged back a poor fellow named Jenkins. Hook and Williams had now reached the last room which gave on to the inner line of defence between the two buildings. Here they found Robert and William Jones fighting off the Zulus, in which they were assisted by two wounded men, Corporal Allan and Private Hitch. Several more wounded men were in the room. There was only one tiny window high up in the wall, which, being an outside one, could not be knocked down like the inside partitions. Each man had to be lifted and pulled through the window, which opened on to the verandah in front, outside the barricade. The men fell to the ground, and some of them were shot or assegaied as they crawled round to get back within the defence line, where Dr. Reynolds did what he could for them under a cloud of assegais. The last sick man, Sergeant Maxfield, was delirious with fever and refused to move. The two Joneses made a last attempt to rescue him, but by now the Zulus were in the room. As they got out, just in time, they saw Maxfield being stabbed.

Of the gallant defence of the hospital, Lieutenant Chard reported: "The garrison of the hospital defended it room by room, bringing out all the sick that could be moved before they retired; Privates Williams, Hook, E. Jones and W. Jones, 24th regiment, being the last men to leave, holding the doorway with the bayonet, their ammunition being expended. From want of interior communication, and the burning of the house, it was impossible to save all. With most heartfelt sorrow, I regret we could not save these poor fellows from their terrible fate."

At sunset, unknown to the defenders, Major Spalding, who was accompanied by Major Upcher and his two companies of the 24th, came within three miles of the mission station, which they saw was burning, thus supporting the assertion, by the native fugitives they had met on the way, that it had fallen. Their further progress barred by a body of Zulus, Major

Spalding ordered his men back to Helpmakaar, the principal advance depot, to protect the large stores of ammunition and food from the Zulu attack which was hourly expected.

To catch up with what had happened while the hospital was being evacuated, we return to the Reverend Smith, who supplies details of the fighting between 4:30 and 6:30 P.M.:

Presently Corporal C. Scammel, Natal Native Contingent, who was near Mr. Byrne, was shot through the shoulder and back; he crawled a short distance and handed the remainder of his cartridges to Lieutenant Chard,* and then expressed his desire for a drink of water; Byrne at once fetched it for him, and whilst giving it to him to drink, poor Byrne was shot through the head and fell dead instantly.

The garden and the road—having the stone wall and thick belt of bush as a screen from the fire of our front defences—were now occupied by a large force of the enemy; they rushed up to the front barricade and soon occupied one side whilst we held the other; they seized hold of the bayonets of our men, and in two instances succeeded in wresting them off the rifles, but the bold perpetrators were instantly shot. One fellow fired at Corporal Schiess, of the Natal Native Contingent (a Swiss by birth, who was a hospital patient), the charge blowing his hat off; he instantly jumped up on the parapet and bayonetted the man, regained his place and shot another, and then, repeating his former exploit, climbed up the sacks and bayonetted a third; a bullet struck him in the instep early in the fight, but he would not allow that his wound was a sufficient reason for leaving his post, yet he has suffered most acutely from it since. Our men at the front wall had the enemy hand-to-hand, and, besides, were being fired upon very heavily from the rocks and caves above us in our rear. Five of our men were here shot dead

* The moment depicted in the well-known painting by Alphonse de Neuville.

[1 3 1]

in a very short space of time; so by 6 P.M. the order was given for them to retire to our retrenchment of biscuit boxes, from which such a heavy fire was sent along the front of the hospital, that although scores of Zulus jumped over the mealie bags to get into the building, nearly every man perished in that fatal leap; but they rushed to their death like demons, yelling out their war-cry of "Usutu, Usutu."

Whilst the hospital was being gallantly defended, Lieutenant Chard and Assistant Commissary Dunne [who, though much exposed, rendered valuable assistance, Chard reported], with two or three men, succeeded in converting the two large pyramids of sacks of mealies into an oblong and lofty redoubt (in the space in front of the store) under heavy fire, blocking up the intervening space between the two with sacks from the top of each, leaving a hollow in the centre for the security of the wounded, and giving another admirable and elevated line of fire all round. About this time the men were obliged to fall back from the outer to the middle, and then to the inner wall of the kraal. The Zulus do not appear to have thrown their assegais at all, using them solely for stabbing purposes.

Lieutenant Bromhead, Smith tells us, led his men in several bayonet charges in an attempt to drive the Zulus away from the hospital, and he states that after it was evacuated,

Corporal Allen and Private Hitch both behaved splendidly. They were badly wounded early in the evening and, incapacitated from firing themselves, never ceased going round and serving out ammunition from the reserve to the fighting men. The light from the burning hospital was of the greatest service to our men, lighting up the scene for hundreds of yards around; but before 10 P.M. it had burned itself out. The rushes and heavy fire of the enemy did not slacken till past midnight, and from that time until daylight a desultory fire was kept up by them from the caves above us in our rear and from the bush and garden in front.

Henry Hook, on his escape from the burning hospital, took the place of a man in the firing line who had been killed, and soon after he had taken up his position, the man next to him was shot through the neck by a bullet which came between the two biscuit boxes behind which they were sheltering. The scene of battle was now brightly illuminated by the flames from the hospital roof, guarding the fort against surprise. In front lay rows of dark corpses, "like waves," says Hook, "for the whirlwind had been checked by fire at a distance of several hundred yards and the Zulus mown down in ranks." Time after time the enemy had been repelled.

The defenders had now withdrawn to the inner redoubt, thus reducing the line of defence to a compact square. Throughout the dark hours of the night, the formidable Undi Corps strained every nerve to complete the capture of the little fort. Often they succeeded in reaching the position, only to be driven back by rifle fire and bayonets.

During a pause in the fighting Hook looked around him. Every soldier, he saw, was at his post. One man crouched by a mealie bag, his rifle pointed at the enemy, his face staring fixedly, like a figure carved in stone. A bright flash of flame disclosed the neat hole in the centre of the man's forehead. Everywhere Hook saw grimy faces, blackened hands, boots sodden with blood, coats, trousers ripped, slashed and stained, twisted bayonets and more than one rifle jammed and useless from repeated firing. Some rifles had broken stocks, for frequently a soldier would have no time to reload his gun, and used his rifle butt to crash over his enemy's head.

Every now and then, says Hook, the Zulus would make a

rush. In the brightly lit scene the defenders did not waste a shot. Again and again the Zulus were repulsed, leaving more and more of their number strewn in front of the barricades. Some passed miraculously unscathed through the murderous fire and managed to climb over the barricade, stabbing and slashing in all directions. They were shot down or driven back by "lung" bayonets (as Hook called them)—bayonets so sharp that many Zulus were pinned to the ground by their terrible thrust.

The Zulus, Hook saw, were massing for another attack, rousing themselves by a war dance. Having goaded themselves to the highest pitch of excitement, they came on, the ground shaking under their charge. Aiming steadily and firing coolly, the defenders shot them down before they could reach the barricades. So heavy was the firing, Hook claims, that the rifles became too hot to hold, the brass cartridges softened and the barrels became foul. He had to stop firing and clean out his rifle with a ramrod. Some barrels of poor quality became twisted and useless.

At last daylight dawned: the long night was over. Looking out, the Reverend Smith saw the Zulus retiring round the shoulder of the hill by which they had approached twelve hours before. Lieutenant Chard ordered out a patrol, setting the rest of the weary men to rebuild the barricades, many sections of which had collapsed, for bullets had ripped open the mealie bags, spilling their contents onto the ground.

Hook marched out, his rifle in one hand, a bunch of assegais over his left shoulder. The ground was strewn with dead Zulus. The leg of one, he noticed, was bleeding profusely. "Dead men don't bleed," he reminded himself. When he went to look closer, the Zulu leaped up, seized the butt of Hook's rifle, trying to drag it from him. The assegais on his shoulder rattled to the ground as the two men struggled for the gun. Suddenly the Zulu relaxed his grip on the rifle and seized Hook's leg, trying to pull him down. "The fight was short and sharp," says Hook; "I struck him in the chest with the rifle butt. The rest was quickly over."

While the patrol was out, the Reverend Smith walked round the walls and barricades, finding dead Zulus piled in heaps, especially in front of the hospital. "About three hundred and fifty dead were subsequently buried by us," he says. The Zulus appear to have carried off their wounded.

Hook returned to the defence line, where, he says, even the most cheerful had no time to dwell on the awful scenes. Seventeen men had been killed, another eight, including Mr. Dalton, the commissariat officer, wounded. The roof of the hospital had fallen in. The Zulus might return at any minute. Why they did not is explained by Mr. J. W. Shepstone, who discussed the battle with many Zulus after the war was over.

The force that attacked Rorke's Drift (so they themselves told me) was the reserve which had not taken part at Isandhlwana. The intention in crossing over into Natal was simply, as they said and I fully believe, to get some cattle. On their way they saw the tents; and, being only three-quarters of a mile away, they made for them. They thus prevented the main body from going any further, as they fought for the greater part of the night and were only too thankful to return quietly next morning across the Buffalo. Here they met Lord Chelmsford and the force with him on the way from Isandhlwana to Rorke's Drift. Some of the officers begged that they might be allowed to attack the force of Zulus; but Lord Chelmsford forbade them attempting anything of the kind. On my telling the Zulus this, in Zululand afterwards, they remarked, "We felt that day that the spirits had watched over us. For, had the white force attacked us, we could have offered only feeble resistance, having had little or nothing to eat the day before, no sleep during the night; whilst having crossed the swollen Buffalo twice, we were completely exhausted."

I asked them whether, had they won the day at Rorke's Drift, they would have gone on into Natal. They replied that they could not have exceeded the king's orders, which were that they were to resist to the utmost in Zululand, but not to invade Natal.

Shepstone points out that this contradicts the generally accepted view in Natal that the successful defence of Rorke's Drift saved the colony from the horrors of Zulu invasion.

It was now 7 A.M. Lieutenant Chard sent a messenger to Helpmakaar asking for help, and posted men with flags on the roof, from where they could see a good distance, to watch for the Zulus and see if there was any sign of relief. "Suddenly we saw the flags waving wildly," says Hook. What was it? Friends or Zulus? Then he noticed that the flags were replying to signals, and he knew they were safe.

Marching mournfully down the road from Isandhlwana towards Rorke's Drift, from where dense columns of smoke could be seen rising from the kraals on the other side of the river, trooper Symons had just enquired of his neighbour, "What has become of our comrades?" when someone shouted, "What is that on the walls?" "It is a man waving a flag," someone called from up in front.

Colonel Russell was sent ahead by Lord Chelmsford to learn if the garrison was really safe, for it was feared that the flag waving might be a Zulu ruse. With him went Norris Newman. As they rode up to the mission house they were greeted by a roar of cheering.

"All right. They are our men," was the welcome news brought back by a mountain trooper. Symons tells us:

Mounting our horses, we quickly crossed the river, and galloped to the punt in order to draw the general and his staff over, after which we handed the rope to the artillery. The native forces got across higher up. On reaching the house, the first body we saw was that of a native auxiliary who was shot for deserting in the hour of need. Around the burned hospital lay in heaps the dead bodies of Zulus. Under the trees in front of the hospital lay three horses still tied to the trunk of a tree. We spent most of the day looking about in the long grass for dead Zulus. Many wounded were found in the orchard and up under the rocks overlooking the house.

Private Hook was making tea when a sergeant came to him to say, "Lieutenant Bromhead wants you." "Wait till I put my coat on," answered Hook. "Come as you are, straight away," he was ordered, and he went in his shirt sleeves with his braces hanging down, to find himself in the presence of Lord Chelmsford and his staff. An officer took down from Hook the story of the defence of the hospital.

When the survivors of the 3rd column marched up, the men were immediately set to work clearing up the mission house and putting it into a state of defence, for no one knew whether the Zulus might attack again. Not until this was completed were rations served out—a boon, says Newman, for men who had been out for two days and nights with nothing to eat or drink except a little biscuit and bad water.

During the afternoon, men of the native contingent were set digging two big holes in front of the hospital for the burial of the 351 dead Zulus, but they positively refused to touch the bodies. The bodies of the fifteen men who fell in the defence of Rorke's Drift were buried in the little cemetery behind the mission, close to the place where they fell, and afterwards a low wall was built to enclose it. Hook tells us that "a bandsman cut a capital picture of the fight" on the stones, using a broken bayonet as a chisel, and that a distinction was made in the burial between those who died in the fight and those who had died of disease. Assistant Commissary Byrne, he says, being a civilian was buried outside the wall.

In his report to Lord Chelmsford, Lieutenant Chard stated:

Of the steadiness and gallant behaviour of the whole garrison I cannot speak too highly. I wish especially to bring to your notice the conduct of Lieutenant Bromhead, 2nd battalion 24th regiment, and the splendid behaviour of his company ("B"); Surgeon Reynolds, Army Medical Department, in his constant attention to the wounded under fire where they fell; acting Commissariat-officer Dalton, to whose energy much of our defences were due, and who was severely wounded while gallantly assisting in the defence; Assistant-Commissary Dunne; acting Storekeeper Byrne (killed); Colour Sergeant Bourne, 2nd battalion 24th regiment; Sergeant Williams, 2nd battalion 24th regiment (wounded dangerously*); Sergeant Windridge, 2nd battalion 24th regiment; Corporal Schiess, 2nd battalion 3rd Natal Native Contingent (wounded); Privates Williams and Jones, 2nd battalion 24th regiment; M'Mahon, Army Hospital Corps; R. Jones and H. Hook, 2nd battalion 24th regiment; and Roy, 1st battalion 24th regiment.

"All behaved so gallantly," says the Reverend Smith, that it was hardly possible to notice other than exceptional instances. "God was very good to us in giving us a little time to get up a defence," Lieutenant Bromhead wrote to his sister in England. "The cool determination displayed by the gallant garrison is beyond praise," stated Lord Chelmsford in his official despatch, and he informed the Secretary of State for

* Williams died a few days later.

War, "The defeat of the Zulus at this post and the very heavy loss suffered by them has to a great extent neutralised the effects of the disaster at Isandhlwana, and it no doubt saved Natal from a serious invasion."

Outnumbered by more than 20 to 1, the little garrison had beaten off repeated attacks of the fiercest description and inflicted terrible losses on the Zulus. Their gallantry was recognised by the award of no less than eleven Victoria Crosses: to Lieutenants Chard and Bromhead; Corporals William Allen and Schiess; Privates Henry Hook, John Williams, William Jones, Robert Jones, Frederick Hitch; and Assistant Commissary J. L. Dalton. For his bravery in attending to the wounded under fire and in voluntarily conveying ammunition from the store to the defenders of the hospital, whereby he exposed himself to a cross fire from the enemy both going and coming, Surgeon Maj. James Henry Reynolds was also awarded a Victoria Cross.

Seldom has the bravery of so few been so conspicuously rewarded.

12

WHOSE DISASTER?

THE FUGITIVES poured into Helpmakaar all evening on January 22. Those who were frightened enough and had any strength left hurried on to escape the Zulu attack, which everyone expected. "We sat up all night momentarily expecting attack," says Mr. Brickhill. Smith-Dorrien struggled in on foot, thankful to find a small garrison commanded by Captain Huntley, who, with Essex, Cockrane, Curling and Gardner, was busy putting the post in a state of defence. Smith-Dorrien says:

I at once took command of one face of the laager, and shall never forget how pleased we weary watchers were when, shortly after midnight, Major Upcher's two companies of the 24th with Heaton, Palmes, Clements and Lloyd, came to reinforce. These two companies had started for Rorke's Drift that afternoon, but had been turned back to Helpmakaar by Major Spalding, a Staff Officer, as he said Rorke's Drift had been surrounded and captured, and that the two companies would share the same fate. Luckily, his information proved to be wrong. I had had a long enough stay, having been on the move, including a stretch of twenty miles on foot, much of it at a run, for forty-two consecutive hours, and directly

[140]

Lieutenant Clements told me he had relieved me, I lay down then and there on two sacks of grain and was fast asleep in a second.

Next day Capt. W. H. Stafford and Lieutenant Davis rode to carry the terrible news to Pietermaritzburg and warn the colonists of the danger of a Zulu invasion. Smith-Dorrien rode to Rorke's Drift, twelve miles away, to resume charge of his transport depot, finding his wagons looted and riddled by bullets. The bodies of dead Zulus and cattle lay everywhere. "Such a scene of desolation," he says, that, to his young mind, it seemed impossible that order could ever be restored. Two dead Zulus, he saw, were hanging on the gallows he had ordered to be rigged for the drying of wagon reins, and he was accused by Major Clery of having ordered them to be lynched. He was exonerated, however, when it was learned that the Zulu warriors had been executed by some of the men, bitter at the loss of their comrades. Other incidents of this sort occurred in the next few days, declares Smith-Dorrien, before law and order were restored. According to Miss Frances Colenso, the daughter of the Bishop of Natal, close to twenty prisoners, after being released and told to run for their lives, were shot down in sight of the whole force. An officer eyewitness told her that there were "not more than seven, nor less than five." He heard the shots and saw the men of the native contingent shooting and stabbing them, which, as Miss Colenso pointed out, was hardly calculated to incline the Zulus to treat *their* prisoners well.

Captain Stafford and Lieutenant Davis reached Pietermaritz-burg, seventy-five miles from Helpmakaar, at dawn on January 24. They rode straight to the government house and roused Sir Bartle Frere. The High Commissioner's immediate reaction to the disastrous news is unrecorded. It was a terrible blow to his high hopes of crushing the barbarian despot. Natal lay at Cetewayo's mercy. If Frere had been right in believing that Cetewayo was only awaiting a favourable opportunity to launch his "celibate man-slaying machine" on Natal, now was the time for him to strike. Only a Zulu invasion could justify Frere's charges against Cetewayo, to stop whose invasion of Natal he had launched a preventive war. But what was his position if Cetewayo missed this golden opportunity? These thoughts must have raced through Frere's mind as he listened to the tale of disaster.

A cable was despatched at once to inform the Prime Minister of the disaster. It took three weeks to reach London, arriving on February 11, having been carried from Cape Town by the *Dunrobin Castle*, which called at the Cape Verde Islands, the southern extremity of the submarine cable, instead of Madeira, thereby saving four days. The Cabinet met at once, and orders were given for the immediate despatch of reinforcements for Natal. Against their wishes Frere had gone to war with Cetewayo. Recriminations could come later; now he had to be supported. Announcing the "Defeat of the British," *The Times* declared, "The power of Cetewayo must be broken." The dead could not be brought back to life, it stated, but "swift and terrible retributions must be exacted." The Zulus, *The Times* pointed out, had proved themselves even more formidable than the military authorities had anticipated. The *Pall Mall Gazette* criticised the "ready-money principle" on which British wars were conducted. The *Daily News*, the opposition organ, said:

> Even those who considered the invasion of Zululand justifiable must be sensitive to the disgrace of beginning a war of the nation's own deliberate seeking in such a manner as to lead to a gratuitous sacrifice of lives, besides imperilling the safety of the possession to safeguard which

the war was professedly undertaken. Death has prematurely visited hundreds of peaceful and happy homes in England. British treasure and blood will now be expended on a scale the authors of the war had not contemplated, and burdens, heavy in all cases and ruinous in many, will be inflicted on struggling industries, and all for what? Lord Beaconsfield's answer is awaited.

Speaking in the House of Lords that evening, Disraeli, the Earl of Beaconsfield, had no further information to give about the disaster at Isandhlwana, but he was able to announce the news of the glorious defence of Rorke's Drift, which "proved that the stamina of the English soldiery has not diminished or deteriorated."

When the news of Isandhlwana became known, all Europe laughed at Britain's discomfiture. Britain's military ineptitude had been proved again—this time by an army of naked savages in a minor colonial campaign, the type of war in which the British had considerable experience and ought to know how to conduct. The British themselves shrugged off the disaster; we always win the last battle, they comforted themselves. Amongst the people the disaster at Isandhlwana was overshadowed by the success at Rorke's Drift, about which a gentleman named Clarence composed an eleven-verse poem. Disraeli, who was struggling to recover from influenza, had a serious relapse. "I am greatly stricken. Everyone was congratulating me on being the most fortunate of Ministers, when there comes this horrible disaster," he complained to Lady Bradford. Mr. Gladstone, the Leader of the Opposition, accused the Prime Minister of spending the taxpayers' money to invade the peaceful homes of an Arcadian people and to kill Zulus, "who in defence of their own land offered their naked bodies to the terribly improved artillery and arms of modern science."

In Natal the news of the terrible disaster spread like wildfire. "It came like a thunder-clap out of a clear blue sky," records one resident. The colonists were incredulous, dumbfounded that a British camp, defended by rifles and artillery, could be overwhelmed by naked savages. Incredulity gave way to grief, fear, dread and panic. A hundred young colonists had perished; the native allies had bolted. The British army had been routed. The triumphant Zulus would now invade Natal, if only in retaliation for the invasion of their land. Lord Chelmsford had stepped on the wasps' nest stirred up by Sir Bartle Frere. He had gone out to scotch the dangerous snake and had been badly bitten. Even now the snake might be coiling to strike back. That Frere himself shared these anxieties is evident from his despatch, written on February 12.

> It has become painfully evident that the Zulu king has an army at his command which could almost any day unexpectedly invade Natal; and owing to the great extent of the frontier, an utter helplessness of the undisciplined hordes of Natal natives to offer effectual resistance, the Zulus might march at will through the country, devastating and murdering, without a chance of being checked, as long as they abstained from attacking the entrenched posts of Her Majesty's troops, which are from 50 to 100 miles apart. The capital and all the principal towns are at this moment in "laager," prepared for attack, which even if successfully resisted, would leave two-thirds of them in ashes, and the country around utterly desolated.

The news of the gallant defence of Rorke's Drift, when it reached Pietermaritzburg, allayed the panic temporarily, but Norris Newman, reaching the town on the afternoon of the twenty-fifth found the most intense excitement prevailing, due to the alarming rumours that had been spread in the absence of reliable information. The townspeople, he found, were expecting a Zulu impi to come charging over the horizon at any moment, and they were actively engaged in laagering the town, constructing barricades, loopholing windows, digging wells and forming themselves into volunteer corps. Every male capable of bearing arms was issued with a rifle and forty rounds of ammunition, and the government records were removed to the jail, the town's strongest building. One lady in delicate health was provided, without her knowledge, with a stretcher laid ready outside her window to carry her to a place of safety. Throughout Natal, isolated colonists packed their goods onto wagons and, driving their stock before them, departed for the nearest town. This state of tension lasted for two months.

The Transvaal Boers, though they themselves were placed in no less danger, expressed, in the words of a Natal colonist, "a very disloyal spirit." Many had secretly hoped that the Zulu campaign would end disastrously, and provide them with an opportunity to throw off British rule. To the Boers the British defeat was good news. The glorious defence of Rorke's Drift was looked upon as no more than an act of Zulu forbearance.

Lord Chelmsford, looking, according to Frere, "many years older, so changed and worn by anxiety and sleeplessness," arrived in Pietermaritzburg on January 26. The campaign was at a standstill. In ten days from the commencement of operations, the whole plan of campaign had fallen through; the Commander in Chief had been surprised and defeated, and had lost half his men and the whole of his reserve ammunition, arms, clothing and food. The right and left columns, those commanded by Colonel Wood and Colonel Pearson, which had advanced into Zululand simultaneously with the centre column, were completely isolated. The invasion of Zululand was abruptly halted. Now the disaster of Isandhlwana had to be explained.

Somebody had blundered. But who? Lord Chelmsford set

up an inquiry, which, he informed the Secretary of State for War, would, he trusted, "be able to collect sufficient evidence to explain what at the present seems to be almost incomprehensible." He told the Secretary of State that Colonel Durnford had been ordered "to move up to strengthen the force which had been left to guard the camp," and that "Lieutenant-Colonel Pulleine was left in charge of the camp and received strict instructions he was left there to defend it."

Describing the battle for the camp, Lord Chelmsford stated: "When the Zulus got round the left flank of these brave men, they appeared to have lost their presence of mind and to have retired hastily through the tents which had never been struck. Immediately the whole Zulu force surrounded them; they were over-powered by numbers and the camp was lost." This was hardly a fair description of the gallant stand of the men of the 24th.

In conclusion Lord Chelmsford made this remarkable statement:

Had the force in question but taken up a defensive position in the camp itself, and utilised there the materials for a hasty entrenchment which lay near to hand, I feel absolutely confident that the whole Zulu army would not have been able to dislodge them. It appears that the oxen were yoked to the wagons three hours before the attack took place, so that there was ample time to construct that wagon laager which the Dutch in former days understood so well. Had, however, even the tents been struck, and the British troops placed their backs to the precipitous Isandhlwana Hill, I feel sure that they could have made a successful resistance.

In other words, Pulleine and Durnford had failed to take the elementary precaution which he, Lord Chelmsford, the over-all commander of the camp, had omitted on each of the nights he occupied it.

Frere backed up Lord Chelmsford. The reasons for the disasters were, he reported to London, the disregarding of Lord Chelmsford's order to laager the camp and not to move out of it in his absence.

So far Lord Chelmsford had made no allegations against Colonel Durnford, nor had he yet stated that Durnford was in command of the camp and therefore responsible for the disaster. But the Natal *Witness* states that it was well known that members of Lord Chelmsford's staff came to Pietermaritzburg prepared to make Colonel Durnford bear the whole responsibility.

The court of inquiry, stigmatised by war correspondent Archibald Forbes as a "solemn mockery," convened on January 27, for four days hearing evidence from survivors of the disaster. The duty of the court, its members were told, was to ascertain what orders had been given for the defence of the camp and how these orders had been carried out. Thus the court was to limit its enquiry strictly to the loss of the camp, and was not to look into "the circumstances of the disastrous affair of Isandhlwana," as Colonel Harness, one of its members, later described it. Lord Chelmsford's actions before and after the disaster were not allowed to be questioned.

In the report of the inquiry, sent to London, which Norris Newman says was "palpably written to establish a preconceived theory," it was stated that Colonel Pulleine had been ordered to defend the camp and that Colonel Durnford had been ordered to move up and take command of it. Therefore, on taking over he was automatically subject to the orders given to Pulleine. Lord Chelmsford's orders had been disregarded. The camp was in a defensive position when Durnford proceeded to act in a manner contrary to the General's orders. Pulleine, being junior to Durnford, was powerless to do more than protest against his troops being taken from the camp he had been ordered to defend. Durnford had moved out of the camp contrary to orders, thus denuding it of its defenders. If Lord Chelmsford's orders had been obeyed, the camp could have been held against the whole Zulu army. Durnford was solely to blame for the disaster. The words "take command of it" crept into the evidence solely on the basis of Colonel Crealock's recollection of the order sent to Durnford, words which were not subsequently found in his notebook when it was picked up on the field of battle.

In forwarding the report to London, Lord Chelmsford informed the Secretary of State for War, "The Court has very properly abstained from giving an opinion, and I myself refrain also from making any observation, or from drawing any conclusions from the evidence therein recorded." But Frere said it for him, describing Isandhlwana in a cable to London as "poor Durnford's disaster."

And as "poor Durnford's disaster" it has been known ever since. He had been in command of the camp and, according to military custom, he was bound by the orders given to Colonel Pulleine to stay in the camp and defend it. Instead, he had further weakened its defences and allowed his detachments to be slaughtered in detail.

Who was truly to blame—Durnford, Pulleine or Chelmsford? The argument has raged for eighty years. The facts are simple: the camp was taken unawares by an unexpectedly large force of Zulus, whom no one thought to be in the vicinity; its loss was due to the line of defence's being too far extended and to the failure of ammunition at the vital moment. The campsite, it is claimed, was badly chosen, and Lord Chelmsford rendered it vulnerable by failing to laager or entrench it, and by sub-dividing his force. Durnford denuded it of defenders by dis-obeying the orders given to Pulleine, to which on reaching the camp he became automatically subject. Then Pulleine fur-ther extended the line when he should, at the first hint of danger, have reduced it and formed a laager.

Fundamentally, there can be no argument as to who was at fault. The blame lies squarely on Lord Chelmsford, who, in his plan of campaign, violated a basic military and strategic prin-ciple, the principle of concentration, by dividing his forces into three columns, with a fourth in reserve, in the face of a numer-ically superior and more mobile enemy. If he had entered Zulu-land in one column, 17,000 men strong, he could not have been defeated. His progress might have been slow, but he could have subjugated the country by the ponderous weight of his advance. This method would have lessened the danger of con-tinual subdivision of his forces, due to the necessity for pro-gressing in hops. Chelmsford could then have established a fresh camp and at the same time protected the old one, for he would have had four times as many men at his disposal.

He claimed that an advance in three columns was necessary in order to protect Natal from invasion, to stop the Zulus from creeping round the rear of one large column, crossing the frontier and massacring the unprotected people of Natal. That was Frere's constant fear, one that no doubt became im-parted to Chelmsford. On Chelmsford's behalf, too, it has been asserted that he allowed himself to be jockeyed into invading Zululand at the wrong time of the year—during the rainy season—by Frere, who was anxious to get the war over before the government in London could stop him. Military com-manders have fallen foul of political expediences before and since, and it was not in Chelmsford's character to stand up to

Frere's entreaties. There is no evidence that he saw any dangers in his plan of campaign, and he entered into the war with complete misunderstanding of the capabilities of the Zulus. He did not listen to the warnings given him, and he plunged headlong to disaster.

But, even so, disaster might have been averted if Chelmsford had obeyed his own orders. The choice of Isandhlwana as a campsite was not intrinsically bad, "inherently vicious" though Archibald Forbes dubbed it. The centre column, of necessity, was forced to advance in easy stages, and Isandhlwana represented the most suitable site for the first hop of the advance. The ground in front was perfectly open for a distance of 800 yards, and the hills to the north were 1,300 yards away. The position was thus uncommanded from any point, and its rear was secured by two hills, Isandhlwana Mount itself and Stoney Hill. "There never was a position where a small force could have made a better stand," stated Lord Chelmsford. But he failed to entrench it, or put the camp into laager. "Not a sod was turned at Isandhlwana," remarks young Smith-Dorrien, who adds: "Had our magnificent body of men been entrenched, the Zulus would have been driven off, and, even as it was, they would have been repulsed in the open had not ammunition run short."

Lord Chelmsford ignored the advice he had received from the experienced Boer leaders. He underestimated the boldness of the Zulus, their amazing mobility and their ability at concealment. His greatest fault lay in his failure to grasp, despite repeated warnings, that the Zulu impi was expected from Ulundi, that 20,000 Zulus lay hidden five miles from the camp he so confidently left early on the morning of the twenty-second. That could, and should, have been discovered by adequate scouting, and that was Lord Chelmsford's responsibility.

[150]

Both Durnford and Pulleine share some of the blame. Whether or not Durnford was ordered "to take command" of the camp, he became its commander by seniority on his arrival. Both he and Pulleine knew that, and Pulleine submitted himself to Durnford's authority. At the moment when Durnford reached Isandhlwana, the camp forces were not unduly extended. Durnford proceeded to extend them by sending Cavaye's company and Raw's Basutos to the hills to the north; and, later, Pulleine, in an attempt to support Cavaye's company, further weakened the defence line.

Then Durnford himself moved out of camp. His failure to stay in the camp and defend it, according to the orders he had inherited from Pulleine, was Chelmsford's apologia for the disaster. All would have been well if Durnford had remained in the camp. But is this true? The presence of his 450 natives could hardly have made much difference to the result, once the initial mistakes had been made. Durnford's rash advance to the southeast precipitated the attack on the camp that would otherwise have been delayed until dawn next day, when it might have been even more disastrous. Lord Chelmsford would have returned with a small escort, and the annihilation of the sleeping British camp could have been achieved by the Zulus without the appalling loss of life that, as it turned out, destroyed their will to win the war. The death of the British commander would have been an even greater feather in their cap.

Durnford was too anxious to get to grips with the Zulus, "brave to the point of rashness," as Frere called him. In his decision to seek out and attack the Zulus reported on the hills to the north, Durnford had the support of Lord Chelmsford's directive, which stated, "If a force remains on the passive defensive, without endeavouring by means of scouting in small bodies, or by raiding in large ones, to discover what the enemy is doing in its immediate front, it deserves to be surrounded and overpowered." Durnford did not know that the whole Zulu army lay before him, and he had every reason to think that before Lord Chelmsford marched out of the camp, he would have ensured that there were no large bodies of Zulus in the vicinity. The order Durnford received that morning told him that Lord Chelmsford had gone out to attack a Zulu force twelve to fourteen miles away.

Pulleine, with the Zulus charging from all directions, failed to withdraw nearer to the tents, possibly because it was already too late, and form a more compact line in the centre of the camp. The forces at his disposal, six companies of the 24th, two guns, a contingent of natives and various mounted colonials, were inadequate to defend an area of 3,000 yards' circumference. Lord Chelmsford's accusation that Pulleine failed to form the wagons at the rear into a laager is hardly valid; it was too late, and the error had already been committed. The gravest charge against Pulleine must inevitably be that he failed to ensure an adequate supply of ammunition to the firing line. That was his responsibility. Whether or not lack of cartridges at a critical moment was a direct cause of the disaster must always remain uncertain. Undoubtedly the Zulus had been checked, their charge halted, when the ammunition failed. But while the Zulu chest was held up, its horns were working round to the left and right of the camp. Even if the men of the 24th had been able to keep up their devastating volley firing, they might have been taken from the rear. Another contributory cause of the disaster, the collapse of the native contingent at the apex of the triangle, was due to an inherent fault: the mistaken policy of employing inadequately armed natives in a campaign against their own cousins, warriors of whom they stood in dread.

Whatever were the faults of his subordinates, Lord Chelmsford knew that he was responsible. On February 9, he asked to be recalled. The strain of prolonged anxiety, as he told the Commander in Chief, the Duke of Cambridge, was too much for him. He requested that an officer of the rank of major general be sent to South Africa at once. Then, three days later, he received a message from Queen Victoria which told him: "The Queen has graciously desired me to say she sympathises most sincerely with you in the dreadful loss which has deprived her of so many gallant officers and men and that Her Majesty places entire confidence in you and in her troops to maintain our honour and our good name."

It gave Lord Chelmsford fresh heart.

13

THE FATAL FIELD

THE FATAL FIELD of Isandhlwana was visited twice by British troops and war correspondents, on March 14 and June 20. Several of the officers and newspapermen described the scene of horror, still dimly discernible in a few old photographs.

Norris Newman of the London *Standard* was present on both occasions. Riding round the Mount, "a horrible scene of desolation was spread before us," he says. He sought to identify the incidents and phases of the battle; all the tents had been burnt, their canvas cut up and taken away, only the poles being left. Everything of value had been looted; scattered about he found sponges, books, brushes, papers and photographs. Walking with him, Captain Symons of the Natal Native Contingent picked up a large bundle of his own cheques. Horses and mules lay dead, still tied to piquet ropes and wagons. The bodies of soldiers lay all about the camp and down the fugitive road, but there were none in Durnford's donga, showing that while his men held it they suffered no loss. The greatest number of bodies in one place, Newman found, was sixty-eight, the majority of whom were men of the 24th. All were horribly decayed. Some were perfect skeletons; others, those that had not been stripped, were "quite unapproachable." The stench was sickening. Try as he might, Newman could not recognise anyone.

Three months later, on his second visit, Newman records,

I found the whole site of the conflict over-grown with grass, thickly intermixed with green and growing stalks of oats and mealies. Concealed among these, lay the corpses of our soldiers, in all postures and stages of decay; while the site of the camp itself was indicated by the debris of the tents, intermingled with a heterogeneous mass of broken trunks, boxes, meat-tins, and their contents, with confused masses of papers, books, letters etc. scattered in wild disorder. The sole visible objects, however, were the waggons, more or less broken up, and the skeletons of horses and oxen. All else was hidden from view, and could only be found by a close search. I had the melancholy satisfaction of discovering my own tent, or rather the disjecta membra of what had once been mine; and immediately behind it were the skeletons of my horses, with the bodies of my servants, just as I had left them piquetted on the 22nd January, when I accompanied the reconnoitring force with Lord Chelmsford. But I could find nothing of any value remaining; my papers, letters and books were lying about, torn up. I found, and brought away with me as mementoes, some of my wife's letters, a book of some of my MS stories, and a photograph that had reached me just two days before the massacre.

Newman joined the search for Durnford's body, which was found by Captain Shepstone. It was surrounded by the bodies of the brave young colonists who had joined him in a last gallant stand and had perished with him. Having known them all well, Newman felt unequal to a minute examination, and he quickly left that part of the field. Their bodies, he says, were covered with stones in default of better burial, as were those of the artillerymen and Natal Military Police. But the bodies of the men of the 24th were left where they lay, at the express desire of Colonel Glyn, who hoped that the regiment might some day be able to render the last sad honours to their dead comrades—a feeling that merited respect, says Newman.

One of the officers present on this melancholy occasion, in a letter quoted by Newman, gives this description:

> There are no skeletons, every body has the skin drawn tightly over the bones. The amount of valuable property destroyed is painful; there are over fifty waggons lying scattered all over the place, some in most extraordinary positions where the oxen had run away with them, and a most wonderful amount of miscellaneous property, papers and books no end—this too after the place has been visited over and over again by parties of men whose looting propensities are proverbial. Hundreds of tins of preserved meats, milk, jam, etc. perfectly uninjured, are kicking about the place, and hundreds of others just pierced by assegais. Brushes and boots are a feature. It really is astonishing the amount of things it is thought necessary for a British army to drag about with them.

Colonel Black, commanding the burial party, which included 140 men of the 2nd Battalion 24th Regiment, and Major Dartnell, who had made the first contact with the Zulus on January 21, reported that the bodies of the slain lay thickest in the camp of the 1st Battalion, where an eyewitness told him he had seen a compact body of the 24th fighting, surrounded by Zulus. Colonel Black counted seventy dead there. Lower down the hill he found another clump of sixty-eight bodies, among them Captain Wardell and Lieutenant Dyer, the bodies of another captain and lieutenant being unrecognisable. Another sixty bodies lay under the southern precipice of Isandhlwana, among them those of Captain Younghusband and two other officers, who looked as though they had held the crags and fought as long as their ammunition lasted. Proof of hand-to-hand fighting was frequent; three soldiers and three Zulus lay confronting each other. Near by was the body of a British redcoat lying face downward with a Zulu knife up to its haft in his back, evidently plunged in from behind while he was defending his front. Beside him Colonel Black picked up two assegais, both bent double. Lower down the slope lay a Natal policeman and a Zulu, still locked in each other's embrace; a few yards away a Zulu skull pierced by a bayonet, a few yards farther on a white man, a rusting assegai pinned to his breast. Amongst the rocks was a Zulu chief, covered by his shield and swathed in four wrappings of canvas, dressed for burial by his men and forgotten in their hurry to get away. Below the precipice of Isandhlwana, Colonel Black came on two bodies, both soldiers of the 24th, one whose shattered skull revealed that he had fallen or been hurled from the top of the Mount, the other still clutching a tent mallet, the feeble club he had matched against his assailant's assegai.

Leaving the field of battle behind him, Colonel Black walked over the neck to search the fugitives' road, to him the saddest sight of all, the place where the routed troops, hoping to survive, set out to run the Zulu gauntlet. The fatal trail was marked by bodies, indicating how dearly the fugitives had sold their lives, how fiercely fighting they fell. Two miles, says Colonel Black, represented the limit reached by white men on foot. The trail continued on to the river bank and ran across it to where the graves of Melville and Coghill marked its end.

Capt. Thomas Shepstone—brother of Sir Theophilus and uncle of Capt. George Shepstone, who lost his life with Colonel Durnford—searched with Jabez for Durnford's body.

Jabez tells the story of finding the body of his beloved leader in a most touching way:

> Captain Shepstone and I had been looking for a long time before we found him. All the rest were getting waggons and caring nothing; and I was a long way off when I heard Captain Shepstone shouting and saw him waving his arm to me to come. And when I came, he said, "Look, Jabez, whose face is this?" and I cried out, for it was he, and I saw my master's face again, just himself unchanged but very little; no one could doubt for a moment. I cut down a waggon-sail with my knife, for we had not even our blankets with us, and I wrapped my chief in it, and I took him up in my arms—it was these hands that touched him—and I carried him gently to the hollow where we laid him.

Before the burial, Shepstone found on the Colonel's body two gold rings and a pocket knife with his name on it, which he sent to the Bishop of Natal for transmission to Durnford's aged mother, to whom the Colonel had written so often and so vividly of his life in South Africa. With Shepstone was Mr. Longeast, the veterinary surgeon and interpreter, who noticed a bullet fall from Durnford's body as they lifted it. A few days later he told a reporter of the Natal *Witness*, "I have not the slightest doubt in my mind but that he was shot through the heart. If you look at the bullet carefully you will observe an impression running round it which was caused by being fired from an old-pattern gun which the Zulus used, and [which] carry very large Kaffir bullets."

Two other visitors to the fatal field were Melton Prior, war artist of the *Illustrated London News*, and Archibald Forbes, of the *Daily News*, freshly arrived in Zululand from Afghanistan, both veterans of many campaigns in Europe. Prior called the field of Isandhlwana the saddest he had seen in all the campaigns he had followed as a war artist, the one he would never forget.

He found himself walking amidst the corpses of many men he knew—the bodies lying amongst the wagons and tents, surrounded by letters from wives, fathers and mothers, photographs and homely little things, their skeletons blackened under the tropical sun, the skull of one with the skeleton of another. One he recognised by a ring, another by a shoulder button. To see at all he had to push the bones aside with a lance, "a sacrilege no doubt," he says, but one he excused by reminding himself, "This is time of war."

Archibald Forbes told his English readers, and the friends and relatives of the dead, how he stumbled over skeletons that rattled to the touch. Here lay a corpse with a bayonet jammed into its mouth up to the socket, transfixing the head and mouth a foot into the ground. There lay a form that seemed cosily curled in calm sleep, turned almost on its face, but seven assegai stabs had penetrated the back. Most of the bodies, says Forbes, lay flat on their back, with the arms stretched widely out and the hands clenched. Most bizarre of all was a dead man lying under a wagon with his head on a saddle for a pillow and a tarpaulin drawn over him, as if he had gone to sleep and died.

Forbes found it miserable work wandering about the desolate camp amid the sour odour of stale death, and he says the scene was sadder and more full of weird desolation than anything he had ever gazed upon. Sitting in his tent that night, he wrote: "There was none of the stark, blood-curdling horror of a recent battle-field; no pools of yet wet blood; no torn flesh still quivering. Nothing of all that makes the scene of a yesterday's battle so repulsive shocked the senses. A strange dead calm reigned in this solitude of nature. Grain had grown luxuriously round and under the waggons, sprouting from the seed that had dropped from the loads, fallen on soil fertilised by the life-blood of gallant men. So long in places had grown the grass that it mercifully shrouded the dead, who for four long months had been scandalously left unburied." In a patch of long grass, near the right flank of the camp, lay Colonel Durnford's body, a central figure in a knot of brave men who had fought it out around their chief to the bitter end. A stalwart Zulu, covered by his shield, lay at the Colonel's feet. Around him, their bodies riddled by assegai stabs, were fourteen Natal Carabineers, with their officer Lieutenant Scott and twenty mounted police. Clearly they had rallied round Colonel Durnford, Forbes saw, in a last despairing attempt to cover the flank of the camp, and had stood fast from choice, when they might have essayed to fly for their horses, which were close by their side at the piquet line. With this group were about thirty gallant fellows of the 24th. In other places men of the 24th were found as if fallen in rallying squares, and there were bodies scattered all along the front of the camp.

The dead, says Forbes, lay as they had fallen, for "strange to relate, the vultures of Zululand that will reduce a dead ox to a skeleton in a few hours, had apparently never touched the corpses of our ill-fated countrymen." As he traced the fitful line of flight by the ghastly token of skeletons, he came upon blackened features and beards blanched by rain and sun, the clothes having lasted better than the poor bodies they covered. Still following the trail of death, Forbes reached the neck. Here the dead lay thick, the string of corpses a broad belt; on the bare ground beyond, the dead were less thick. Many there, Forbes noted, wore the uniform of the Natal Mounted Police. Crossing the bed of a rocky stream, he came to a precipitous ravine, on its edge a jammed gun limber whose horses in their harness hung over its steep face. A little farther on, there was a broken ambulance wagon, around it the bodies of the poor fellows who had been torn off and stabbed to death.

No cross or stone marks the individual graves of those who fell at Isandhlwana, the obelisk unveiled in 1914 to the memory of the men of the 24th serving as a monument to them all. But above their last resting places rises the most fitting monument of all, the craggy rock itself, conspicuous for twenty miles around, shaped so strangely like the regimental badge of the 599 officers and men of the 24th Foot whose presence there in death makes that little spot in faraway Zululand forever part of England. There the honoured dead rest: the young lieutenant from the Lincolnshire country rectory, the boy from the Birmingham slum, the youthful colonist from Natal, the native conscript, side by side with the Zulu warrior who died in defence of his land. Their names are forgotten, as are the cries of those who mourned them long, long ago.

14

FAILURES AND SUCCESSES

CETEWAYO did not invade Natal. He kept his impis strictly within their own borders. His warriors had done what they set out to do; they had driven the central invading column back over the frontier and disorganised the others. "We have done well. That is one column we shall not hear of again," said Cetewayo. Having done their duty, his warriors returned to their homes to mourn their dead, lick their wounds and enjoy their plunder. There was no provision for the impi to remain permanently mobilised, no national commissariat department to keep it on a war footing. But it was soon to be in action again.

Cetewayo was angry with Dabulamanzi for crossing the Buffalo River and raiding Rorke's Drift. Dabulamanzi's royal blood alone saved him from execution. The king told Cornelius Vijn, the young Dutchman who remained unharmed at Cetewayo's kraal throughout the war, that he was glad of his victory, but angry that a regiment had crossed the river. "It is the whites who have come to fight with me in my own country and not I that go to fight with them," he told him.

In Natal considerable ingenuity was shown in explaining why Cetewayo, in Lord Chelmsford's words, "missed his opportunity." Frere put down his failure to take advantage of the defencelessness of the colony to the "half-heartedness of a suspicious barbarian despot." That the triumphant Zulus did not invade them was attributed by the colonists to the flooding of the frontier rivers, the victors' enjoyment of their plunder and the habitual disbandment of a savage army after a great victory.

The evidence indicates that Cetewayo had no wish to invade Natal. His failure to do so when he had the chance suggests that Frere's belief in the Zulu menace was ill founded. Only by taking the war into his enemy's country could Cetewayo hope to save his land from a renewal of the invasion on an overwhelming scale. Only as master of Natal could he extract favourable terms from an imperial government that might then be willing to compromise. The possibility that the British government would extract a terrible vengeance for the invasion of Natal was a remote issue; but if Cetewayo stayed where he was and did nothing, his independence surely had only a few months to run. The invasion of Zululand had merely been postponed. The Zulu chief's only chance of retaining his freedom lay in the utter defeat of the people who had made plain their intention to reduce him to the status of a puppet-king and to destroy Zulu nationalism. By his failure to invade Natal Cetewayo lost the war that had been thrust upon him.

In his letters to London, Frere minimised the disaster at Isandhlwana and glorified the defence of Rorke's Drift, to which he attributed the safety of the colony. Isandhlwana had been no more than an unfortunate setback, due to the failure of some officers to follow orders. His plans were unchanged, but it would now take a little longer to settle the Zulu question. The die for peace or war, he said, had been cast eighteen months before, when the annexation of the Transvaal became known to Cetewayo. "It was then a simple question whether we should steadily bring our differences to an issue on a clear and unmistakable demand for our right to live at peace with our neighbours, or whether we should await the convenience of the Zulu King, and be taken at a disadvantage when he saw his opportunity."

Five days after Isandhlwana Frere told the Colonial Secretary, "You must not think that it will be very difficult to bring the Zulu King to reason. You must strengthen the regular force and effectually crush the Zulu King's power. It is really not so difficult as it seems." He assured Sir Michael Hicks-Beach, "I need not tell you that I came to South Africa on a mission of peace," and he pointed out that a hut tax imposed on the Zulu people would pay for the British administration of their country. "They are an easily manageable people," he told the Colonial Secretary, "if they are not brought up as wolves."

But however nonchalant Frere made himself appear, he must have guessed that the day of reckoning was at hand. Against the expressed wish of the Imperial Government, which in November had been *"most anxious* not to have a Zulu war on its hands," and which had urged Frere to use "all proper means of keeping out of war," he had presented an unacceptable ultimatum and invaded Zululand. If the campaign had been brought to a swift and successful conclusion, Frere's "disobedience" would have been forgotten in the general rejoicing. But the war had started with a terrible, inexplicable disaster. In England both Frere's rashness and the Government's culpability were attacked. The blame had to be shifted to Frere. That was easy to do if the Government adopted the time-honored device of telling the public only half the story.

Government censure was not long delayed. Frere should have obtained the Cabinet's sanction for the terms of the ultimatum. It was not until the Cabinet received it, when it was too late to stop Frere, that Her Majesty's Ministers had any reason to anticipate anything "that could fairly be characterised as an aggressive policy." The Colonial Secretary's despatch stated that the Cabinet

> have been unable to find in the documents you have placed before them that evidence of urgent necessity for immediate action, which alone could justify you in taking, without their full knowledge and sanction, a course almost certain to result in a war, which, as I had previously impressed upon you, every effort should have been made to avoid.
>
> The communications which have passed between us as to the objects for which the reinforcements were requested and sent, and as to the nature of the questions in dispute with the Zulu King, were such as to render it especially needful that Her Majesty's Government should understand and approve any important step, not already suggested to them, before you were committed to it; and, if that step was likely to increase the probability of war, an opportunity should certainly have been afforded them of considering, as well the time, as the manner of coming to issue—should it be necessary to come to issue—with the Zulu King, and though the further correspondence necessary for this purpose might have involved the loss of a favourable season for the operations of the British troops, and might have afforded Cetewayo the means of further arming and provisioning his forces, the circumstances rendered it imperative that, even at the risk of disadvantage, full explanations should be exchanged.

The despatch of censure ended with this statement of governmental opinion; "It is with great regret that they feel constrained to adopt the view which I have expressed of your omission to follow a course which appears to them, for the reasons I have stated, to have been peculiarly incumbent upon you in this instance."

Frere received this despatch on April 25, having been previously warned of its contents by a private letter from Hicks-Beach, who urged him not to resign. "I attach the greatest importance to your continuance in South Africa," he stated.

In his reply Frere developed an ingenious theory. He claimed that if he had not attacked Cetewayo, the Transvaal Boers would have revolted. Delay would have involved risks greater than a Zulu war. The Boers, he stated, would have committed some act of violence, and bloodshed would have been the inevitable result. "What would the Zulus have done?" he asked. "Observed a strict neutrality?" All Cetewayo's power would have been unable to make them observe it, he said. His young men would have "washed their spears" in white men's blood, Dutch or English. The Boer rebellion might have extended to Cape Colony; "Ill blood and life-long race hatred," observed Frere, "certainly would." The Zulu sallies would have been far worse than an inroad on Natal, Frere claimed, and he asked, "How should I have answered you for incurring such a misfortune by shirking the responsibility of bringing Cetewayo to account?" The choice, he declared, was between doing what he did, risking a Zulu war at once, or incurring the risk of what was still worse: "a Zulu war a few months later, preceded by a Boer rebellion."

That was Frere's excuse for attacking Cetewayo when he did. It seems a poor one. Unquestionably, the Transvaal Boers were restive under British rule and were demanding their freedom. Their delegates who had been sent to put the Boers' case before the Cabinet in London had been turned down. They were angry at the terms of the boundary award. They refused absolutely to assist the British against the Zulus. But it is significant that the Boers did not rebel until after the Zulu menace had been scotched. The Boers were unlikely to have risen against the British as long as there was the danger of the Zulus' siding with their enemies, as they certainly would have done.

On another issue Frere was on stronger ground. The Imperial Government had accused him of "disobedience" in starting a Zulu war without its knowledge or consent. For the Cabinet to maintain that they knew nothing of Frere's warlike designs was absurd. Throughout 1878 he had stated his intention of settling the Zulu question once and for all. Up to early October, the Cabinet acquiesced in that policy, saying that Cetewayo must be kept in order and "coerced." The feet in Downing Street grew cold only when affairs in Europe became pressing. The Zulu war must be *"postponed,"* Hicks-Beach wrote on October 7. By the time Frere heard that the Cabinet were *"most anxious* to avoid a Zulu war," the die had been cast.

In London the pressure against Frere was increasing. The vital private letters that had passed between the High Commissioner and the Colonial Secretary were withheld from publication. The "Despatches" printed as "Command Papers" and laid before the Houses of Parliament told an incomplete story.

On May 23, the Cabinet threw Frere to the wolves. He was superseded as High Commissioner responsible for Natal and the Transvaal. Gen. Sir Garnet Wolseley was ordered to South Africa to take his place and that of Lord Chelmsford as Special Commissioner and Commander in Chief. Frere was to remain only as Governor of Cape Colony. Queen Victoria insisted on that. Frere had been made the scapegoat for Isandhlwana; Chelmsford still had a chance to redeem his fortunes. "For God's sake do something. Wolseley supersedes you," cabled his brother, the Lord Chief Justice of England.

Although supersession was a far more serious withdrawal of confidence than the censure of March 13, Frere did not resign. Why he stayed on in South Africa is explained by his biographer, Basil Worsfold: "Frere was prevented from resigning on his censure and supersession by his absolute belief in the rightness of his conduct in Natal, and his unwavering assurance that with the full understanding of the facts the adverse judgement of the Cabinet and of the nation would be reversed."

Frere's removal from the control of affairs in Natal now meant that the Zulus, upon their inevitable defeat, would face treatment quite different from what Frere had intended for them.

Lord Chelmsford's conduct of the Zulu war came in for many criticisms, not the least that, after Isandhlwana, he had continued his campaign with "perverse pedestrianism," as Archibald Forbes jibed. Chelmsford delayed until July giving the *coup de grâce* to Cetewayo. He did so just in time, before Wolseley's arrival could rob him of final victory.

Meanwhile the British defeat at Isandhlwana was followed by two further disasters, which were quickly retrieved by a signal victory.

Immediately following Isandhlwana, Chelmsford concentrated the remainder of his ill-fated third column at Helpmakaar and Rorke's Drift, where it stood solely on the defensive, as did the other two columns. Advancing towards Eshowe, Colonel Pearson's right column was attacked by 5,000 Zulus at

Inyezane on January 22. After a battle that lasted one and a half hours, the Zulus were driven off. The British force lost twelve killed and sixteen wounded, while inflicting 300 casualties on the enemy. Pearson reached the mission station at Eshowe, thirty-six miles inside Zululand, next day, and on learning of the Isandhlwana disaster he went into laager, being invested by a large Zulu force for over two months. Evelyn Wood, commanding the left column, on hearing of Lord Chelmsford's defeat, entrenched himself at Kambula Hill.

Lord Chelmsford's first need was to relieve Eshowe. That took time to organise, and meanwhile the war was at a standstill. The disaster at Isandhlwana, wrote Lord Chelmsford to the Duke of Cambridge, "has thrown back the subjugation of Zululand to an indefinite period." Its effect on the native population of Natal had been great; four out of the seven native battalions had disbanded themselves, and the other three were scarcely to be depended upon. The native contingent, he told the Commander in Chief, would never again be of any use.

The second disaster to the British forces in Zululand came on March 12. Though a minor one, it exemplified, even more than Isandhlwana, the casualness with which the whole campaign was conducted. Capt. R. D. Moriarty had been ordered to escort a convoy of 104 wagons to Luneberg, in northern Zululand, with his company of the 80th Regiment, consisting of 104 men. The convoy, reaching the Intombi River, found it in flood, and by nightfall had ferried across only a few of the wagons. In consequence two camps were formed, one on either bank, a force of thirty men under Lieutenant Harward being sent over the river to guard the wagons on the south bank. Moriarty drew up the bulk of the wagons in a triangular laager with its base on the north bank, where they were further protected by swampy ground on one side. The whole force then

proceeded to retire to its tents for the night, leaving only one
sentry on guard, even though the camp lay under the shadow
of the stronghold of Chief Umbeline, a man of sinister reputa-
tion not inappropriately nicknamed "the Assassin."

A shot from the sentry's rifle at 5:15 A.M. brought the men
on the north bank tumbling out of their tents to find thousands
of Zulus swarming amongst them, yelling "Usutu," stabbing
and firing their guns. Moriarty was killed and his camp overwhelmed in a matter of seconds. Aroused by the sentry's shot,
Lieutenant Harward drew up his men on the other bank, and
under the protection of their fire, twelve of Moriarty's seventy-
one men succeeded in swimming the river, hotly pursued by the
Zulus. Joseph Sussens, a wagon conductor, also succeeded in
escaping. He was fast asleep in his wagon when he became
aware that something unusual was taking place outside. Hearing
shouts and screams, he peered from under the wagon canopy
to see Zulus everywhere. It was time to go, he told himself,
but in the dark he could find neither his rifle nor his clothes.
Remembering that his friend Whittington was asleep in the
next wagon, he crawled to it and called, "Whittington," and
heard the latter's reply, "I'll be down in a jiffy." A second
later Whittington jumped down on the side opposite to
Sussens. There was an awful shriek, and that was the end of
Whittington. Creeping off, clad only in his nightdress, Sussens
got to the river, slipped in unobserved and swam underwater
as long as he could. Surfacing for a second to catch his breath,
he saw that the Zulus were lining the bank, shooting down the
swimmers. He dived again and reached the other bank, emerging without his nightshirt. The Zulus, he saw, were swimming
across and Lieutenant Harward and his men were retreating
towards a farmhouse in the rear.

At this critical stage in the proceedings, Lieutenant Har-

ward saddled his horse and galloped off to Luneberg, to fetch
help, he said later. His men, rallied by Colour Sgt. Anthony
Booth, retreated slowly, holding off the Zulus with accurate
fire. Sussens decided to join them. Entirely naked, he made a
run for it, the Zulu bullets whistling around his ears. He caught
up with two other fugitives, both of whom were shot by his
side as they ran. When he reached Booth, the little force
continued its retreat, which was now blocked by sixty Zulus
who had crossed the river and were threatening their rear.

At this juncture the Luneberg garrison, commanded by
Major Tucker, whom Harward had warned, came galloping
up, and the Zulus retired with their booty. Three of Harward's
men had been killed, making the total loss sixty-two British
and seventeen native wagon drivers. Lieutenant Harward's conduct led to a court-martial, at which he was acquitted of the
charge of abandoning his men at a moment of extreme danger.
But he did not escape official censure, for the Commander in
Chief, the Duke of Cambridge, refused to confirm the verdict,
giving his reasons as follows:

> Had I released this officer without making any remarks
> upon the verdict in question, it would have been a tacit
> acknowledgement that I concurred in what appears to
> me a monstrous theory, viz., that a regimental officer who
> is the only officer present with a party of soldiers actually
> and seriously engaged with the enemy, can, under any
> pretext whatever, be justified in deserting them, and by
> so doing, abandoning them to their fate. The more help-
> less the position in which an officer finds his men, the
> more it is his bounden duty to stay and share their fortune
> whether for good or ill. It is because the British officer
> has always done so that he occupies the position in which
> he is held in the estimation of the world, and he pos-
> sesses the influence he does in the ranks of our army. The

soldier has learned to feel that, come what may, he can in the direst moment of danger look with implicit faith to his officer, knowing that he will never desert him under any possible circumstances.

It is to this faith of the British soldier in his officers that we owe most of the gallant deeds recorded in our military annals; and it is because the verdict of this Court-Martial strikes at the root of this faith, that I feel it necessary to mark officially my emphatic dissent from the theory upon which the verdict has been founded.

Lieutenant Harward was ordered to return to duty, but the Commander in Chief's censure was read at the head of every regiment in Her Majesty's Service. Colour Sergeant Booth was awarded the Victoria Cross.

The next disaster was far worse.

Col. Evelyn Wood, V.C., commanding the left column in northern Zululand, had occupied the weeks of inactivity following Isandhlwana by staging a series of cavalry raids on neighbouring strongholds and kraals, by flying columns led by Col. Redvers Buller, later of Boer War fame. Riding from Wood's fortified camp at Kambula, twelve miles south of Luneberg, the columns killed a number of Zulus, burnt their kraals and drove off their cattle. This so incensed Cetewayo that he sent a message to Wood complaining that he was stealing cattle when he ought to come out into the open and give battle, and warning him that if he stayed at Kambula he would be annihilated. Now Wood received orders from Lord Chelmsford to create a diversion in northern Zululand on March 28, to cover Chelmsford's relief of Eshowe, held by the right column. In consequence, Wood decided to attack Umbeline's stronghold on Inhlobana Mountain, a natural for-

tress protected by narrow defiles, steep precipices and sub-
terranean passages.

Wood divided his flying column into two forces, one commanded by Colonel Buller, with whom rode 400 mounted men
and 300 natives, and the other by Colonel Russell, with whom
went 250 mounted men and 250 natives. Each party was
ordered to climb the mountain from opposite sides. Wood followed with his staff and a small escort.

The ascent of the long, flat-topped mountain was achieved
with great difficulty and some loss. Umbeline's retainers were
driven from their caves and rocky krantzes, their leader was
slain and 2,000 head of cattle were captured and taken to the
plain below by Russell. Then, at 9 A.M., Wood saw 20,000 Zulus
marching across the plain, at a distance of six miles, clearly
intending to encircle the mountain and cut off his retreat. It
was now too late for Buller's men to descend the mountain
by the comparatively easy pass by which they had climbed it.
Their only chance of escape lay in retreating at the other end
by a defile, which his scouts reported was impractical for men
on foot. Meanwhile thousands of Zulus were climbing the
mountain by baboon tracks in his rear and spreading out
across its summit. In the fighting that followed the British
force suffered heavily. Colonel Weatherley, his sixteen-year-
old son, who refused to leave his father, and all his troop of
Colonial Volunteers, consisting of five officers and forty men,
were annihilated; and Piet Uys, the leader of the only Boer
commando in the field, was killed while trying to save the life
of the eldest of his four sons. In all, of Buller's 400 mounted
men, twelve officers and eighty soldiers were killed either then
or in the mad gallop down "Devil's Pass," the one opening not
occupied by the Zulus, a precipitous, boulder-strewn passage,
only wide enough to admit two horsemen abreast. In their

perilous retreat, the troop became a tumbled, jumbled mass, scrambling and slithering down the mountainside. A number of horses and men were forced over the brink and crashed to their death on the rocks below, but Buller by his calmness and bravery succeeded in bringing the survivors down to the plain, from where they galloped back to Kambula—a feat of valour which earned him the Victoria Cross.

One of Weatherley's men, given up for lost, was captured by the Zulus. The story of his final escape is a famous one. This trooper, a Frenchman named Grandier, was taken before Umbeline, who decreed his death, but an old chief insisted that he should be sent to Cetewayo. Forced to march naked for four days, Grandier was brought before the Zulu king, whom he found sitting in his kraal having an English newspaper read to him by an English-speaking native. Around him Grandier saw the two cannon captured at Isandhlwana and a number of Martini–Henry rifles. When Cetewayo learned that Umbeline had been killed at the subsequent battle of Kambula, he ordered that Grandier should be taken back and put to death in revenge. He was escorted by two Zulus, one armed with a rifle. When, on the third day of the journey, the Zulus lay down to rest, Grandier seized an assegai and killed one, whereupon the other made off. Travelling by night and hiding by day, he reached Wood's camp on April 15.

Meanwhile Cetewayo's impi, commanded by his principal induna, Umnyamana, fresh from its triumphs at Inhlobana Mountain, turned on Kambula. A renegade Zulu informed Wood that his camp was to be attacked at "dinnertime" next day, March 29. A herd boy had listened in while the Zulu chiefs were discussing the assault; he told his chief, who informed Wood.

Kambula camp consisted of a wagon laager, 200 yards by

150 yards, a redoubt 150 yards to the east and a small cattle kraal formed of wagons in between and slightly to the south, the whole camp occupying the ridge of a spur of the neighbouring hills. On the north the ground lay completely open, but to the south it fell in abrupt ridges which could provide excellent cover for an attacking force. It was defended by 2,086 men, composed of 110 artillerymen with 6 seven-pound guns and 2 rocket tubes; 11 Royal Engineers; 1,238 British infantry belonging to the 13th and 90th Regiments; and Buller's 727 mounted men.

The Zulus swept into sight at 11 A.M., marching in five columns. Knowing the time of attack, Wood ordered the tents to be struck and reserve ammunition laid out; at 12:45 the men's dinners were served.

Approaching from the east, the Zulu columns split up, the right horn circling round to the north while the chest and left horn moved to the south and west of the camp, clearly intending to take it from four sides simultaneously. It was now 1:25 P.M., and the right horn reached its position far in advance of the chest and left horn. Wood saw his opportunity to precipitate the attack before the Zulus were ready. He despatched Buller with 100 mounted men to the north to attack the right horn, composed of the Nkobamakosi Regiment, which had been given this honor of place in recognition for its losses at Isandhlwana. Commanding a wing was our old friend Mehlokazulu, again busy with his "notebook and pencil" as well as with his rifle. Galloping to within 400 yards of the Nkobamakosi Regiment, Buller halted his men, dismounted and fired. This was more than the brave warriors could resist. They sprang up and charged Buller, who mounted and retreated firing, drawing the Zulus on. Without waiting to see if the chest and left horn were ready the Nkobamakosi Regiment rushed on the camp into which Buller had retreated. In a flash every gun and rifle was turned upon them. Caught in the open, the regiment, exhausted, "so tired, we could do nothing," as Mehlokazulu says, was almost annihilated. "We were prostrate, beaten," explains the ever-truthful eyewitness. The dead lay so thick that each living man was surrounded by bodies. "We lost more men than at Isandhlwana," records Mehlokazulu. The survivors of the regiment retreated to some rocks northeast of the camp, where they stayed, taking no further part in the battle, which now veered to the south.

By 2:15 P.M., the Zulu chest and left horn had occupied the dead ground close to the camp. Two regiments sprang up to charge. The Nokenke Regiment, 1,500 strong, burst into the cattle kraal, driving out a company of the 13th Regiment. The Mbonambi Regiment pushed up the slope towards the main laager, shouting, in place of their usual war cry, "We are the men from Isandhlwana." Wood did not await their assault. He sent out two companies of the 90th Regiment under Major Hackett to meet the Zulus at bayonet point. The British soldiers drove them back with heavy losses, but Hackett himself was severely wounded. Some Zulus, however, succeeded in reaching the main laager, where they tried to seize the muzzles of the defenders' rifles with their bare hands, and they threw the bodies of their own dead onto the points of the bayonets barring their passage. For an hour or so confused fighting continued between the laagers, the Zulus in the cattle kraal inflicting a number of casualties in the redoubt by their enfilading fire. They were driven out by a sortie of two companies of the 13th Regiment. The survivors of the Nokenke and Nkobamakosi Regiments fell back, both virtually annihilated. The two-hour attack on the camp had been beaten off.

But one young Zulu, in retreat, the son of a chieftain, could not resist the temptation to fire a last shot with his new and much-prized Martini–Henry rifle, his loot from Isandhlwana. He stopped, turned around, knelt down and aimed carefully at a British soldier then exposing himself in the wagon laager. But, as it happened, another British soldier had exactly the same idea, to have a last shot at the fleeing Zulus. Observing the kneeling rifleman, he aimed carefully, and just as the young Zulu was about to press his trigger, fired. The bullet severed the Zulu's thumb and smashed the stock of his rifle. He was able, however, to reach a native hut, when he found his commander, Umnya-mana himself, who, recognising him, ordered his hand bound up.

It was now 4:30 P.M. Seeing that the Zulus were wavering, Wood ordered, "Cavalry out," and in an instant Buller's mounted men were thundering over the plain, slashing and cutting at the fleeing and exhausted Zulus. Commander Schermbrucker, commanding the Cape Colony Volunteers, swept round and headed the fugitives off from the Umfolozi River, pushing them towards Buller. Only the onset of dark-ness saved the Zulu impi from complete destruction, says Mehlokazulu. Seven hundred and eighty-five bodies were col-lected and buried, but the Zulu loss must have been nearer 2,000. In the British camp eighteen men had been killed and sixty-five wounded, of whom ten died of their wounds.

Their terrible defeat at Kambula shattered Zulu morale. The great effort launched to drive Colonel Wood from Zulu-land had failed. The Zulus had finally learnt they were no match for British regulars. Cetewayo was furious that the impi had attacked the entrenched laager, which he had expressly ordered it not to do.

While Colonel Wood was engaged in winning the greatest victory of the campaign, Lord Chelmsford was moving up to

relieve Colonel Pearson at Eshowe, bringing with him a force
of 3,390 Europeans, chiefly new regiments recently arrived in
Natal, and 2,280 natives. No precaution was overlooked. Each
night the column went into laager, the encircled wagons being
protected by shallow trenches; the men slept on the sodden
ground ready to spring up in a second at any emergency; spare
ammunition boxes, each provided with its own screwdriver,
were laid out behind each contingent.

On the evening of April 1, the column encamped by the
Gingihlovo stream. All night the rain poured down. At dawn
next morning one of Lord Chelmsford's A.D.C's, scanning the
country around with his field glasses, saw what he thought was
a coffin-shaped black bush. But the bush was moving and there
was no wind. A dense column of Zulus were silently moving
on the camp. By 6 A.M. the Zulus had surrounded the laager,
and were attacking it from all sides. For twenty minutes "these
really splendid savages," as Norris Newman called them, rushed
at the camp with "wonderful pluck." The Zulu regiments, led
by Dabulamanzi, the victor of Isandhlwana, were swept away
by rifle and cannon fire. Inside the laager, records Norris Newman, Lord Chelmsford, "wearing a red nightcap," was everywhere encouraging his men and telling them to fire low and
steadily. With a swirl of their bagpipes, the 91st Highlanders
charged the fleeing Zulus. The cavalry completed the rout.
Eleven hundred Zulu bodies were collected and buried, the
British loss being thirteen dead and forty-eight wounded. By
the British soldiers the site of the battle was named "gin, gin,
I love you." Next day the column relieved Eshowe and brought
the garrison back to Natal.

The clouds that had darkened the opening of the campaign
to bring Cetewayo "to reason" were rolling away.

15

THE FINAL
TRIUMPH

REINFORCEMENTS poured into Natal. The first contingent to arrive was unexpected. When he received the news of Lord Chelmsford's disaster, the Governor of St. Helena persuaded Captain Bradshaw, commanding H.M.S. *Shah*, on her way home after three years' service in the Pacific, to carry a battery of artillery and a company of the 88th Regiment to Durban, where he arrived on March 6, earning the highest praise from the Lords of the Admiralty. Four days later the troopship *Tamar* docked from Ceylon with the "Diehards," the 57th Regiment, on its way home to England. The first of the reinforcements from England arrived early in April on board the Royal Mail steamer *Pretoria*, after a record passage, among them the 91st Highlanders, a Scottish regiment which wore "trews," not kilts. Other ships brought the 1st Dragoon Guards; the 17th Lancers; four major generals; replacements for the 1st Battalion 24th Regiment; a flock of war correspondents; and Louis Eugène Napoleon Bonaparte, aged twenty-two, the son of the late Emperor Napoleon III, called the "Prince Imperial" of France. By April 11 Lord Chelmsford had under his command a force of 17,528 men, consisting of 9,364 British Infantry, 3,957 Colonial Infantry, 1,190 British Cavalry, 1,877 Colonial Horse, 385 Royal Engineers, and 755 Royal Artillerymen with 36 guns.

The arrival of the Prince Imperial to act as an "additional" A.D.C. posed many problems for Lord Chelmsford. The prince had lived in England with his mother, the Empress Eugénie, since his father's abdication, following the disastrous Franco-Prussian war, and Disraeli had been persuaded, much against his will, by Queen Victoria and the empress to allow him to see service in South Africa. "What can you do when you have to deal with two obstinate women?" the Prime Minister desparingly wrote to his friend Lady Chesterfield. Lord Chelmsford was anxious to keep the prince out of harm's way; the prince was equally determined to get into the thick of the war. Chelmsford imposed restrictions on his movements, under which the adventurous young prince chafed. Having great skill at sketching, he was permitted to accompany Wood's flying column in northern Zululand, on condition that he did not take unnecessary risks. Although a minor episode of the campaign, the death of the Prince Imperial in a skirmish on June 1 shocked the world.

Early on that day the prince took out a reconnaissance party composed of six Natal troopers, one Basuto scout and Lieutenant Carey of the 98th Regiment, who asked to be taken along. He left behind the troop of Basuto horse which had been ordered to accompany him. During the afternoon the party reached a deserted Zulu kraal north of the Ngutu Hills, and some eight miles from Isandhlwana, where the prince ordered his troop to offsaddle. While the party was resting, the

Basuto guide became suspicious that there might be Zulus lurking in the long grass only thirty yards from the spot where the prince sat sketching, but he was unable to convey the information to the prince, who did not understand Zulu. At 3:50 P.M. the prince gave orders to saddle up, and the knee halters were taken off the horses. At that moment there came a crash of rifle fire from the long grass. No one was hit, but the horses reared and plunged, so that both the troopers and Carey had the greatest difficulty in mounting, which at last they succeeded in doing. The prince was not so lucky. His horse, a high-spirited grey standing sixteen hands high, became unmanageable, and he found it impossible to mount. He ran alongside it as it followed after the others, making a valiant attempt to vault into the saddle. His tremendous effort would doubtless have proved successful but for the ill luck that, when he grasped one of the stirrups to pull himself into the saddle, the leather broke and he was thrown to the ground. Meanwhile two troopers had been shot and Lieutenant Carey and a trooper had reached a donga about 250 yards away. The other three crossed it at a different point. Then and only then did Carey realise that the prince was not with them. Seeing a number of Zulus at the kraal, he rode on until he met Evelyn Wood, who was now a brigadier general, and Colonel Buller. By then it was getting dark, too late to effect a rescue, if that was still possible, or to recover the prince's body. Next day a party was sent out commanded by Captain Cockrane, one of the survivors of Isandhlwana.

The bodies of the two troopers and that of the Prince Imperial were found where they fell. In his body were eighteen assegai wounds, all in front, and his stomach had been slashed open. By his side lay his little bulldog, also assegaied. Brought back to camp, the body was identified by M. Deleage, the special correspondent of the Paris *Figaro* and by the prince's servant, Xavier Uhlmann, an old family retainer. According to the evidence of eyewitnesses the body was found naked; but a famous story relates that, when the prince was discovered, a bullet wrapped in a newspaper cutting fell from his jacket pocket. Legend has it that when, at the age of fourteen, the prince received his baptism of fire at the battle of Saarbrucken, he picked up as a memento a dud bullet that had fallen beside him. The French newspapers got hold of the story and magnified it as "the bold deed of the young prince." This led to bitter jests, which poisoned the boy's mind, and he kept the bullet and the newspaper cutting, determined one day to show his true worth to the people who had mocked him.

The prince's body was embalmed and taken to England, and in 1880 the Empress Eugénie came to Zululand and was taken by Evelyn Wood to the spot where her son died. Years later, Wood told the publisher of his memoirs that she immediately recognised the place by the presence of a patch of wild violets, the flowers her son loved.

Lieutenant Carey came in for severe condemnation, somewhat unfairly, for his position in the party was ambiguous. Although the prince was in command, Carey was censured for allowing the troop to be surprised. He was sent back to England under arrest for "having been guilty of misbehaviour before the enemy"—a charge that the Commander in Chief advised the Queen was not sustained by the evidence. Nonetheless, the Duke of Cambridge expressed, "with the voice of the army, his regret that, whether or not an attempt at rescue was possible, the survivors of this fatal expedition withdrew from the scene of the disaster without the full assurance that all efforts on their part were not abandoned until the fate of their comrades had been sealed."

It was now mid-June, and Lord Chelmsford was advancing slowly on Ulundi in three columns. As he progressed, messages were brought to him from Cetewayo imploring that an end should be made to hostilities, to which Lord Chelmsford replied: "If Cetewayo wishes for peace he must give substantial proof of being in earnest. He must at once restore all horses, oxen, arms, ammunition and other property taken during the war. One or more regiments, to be named by me, must come under a flag of truce, and, at a distance of 1,000 yards from my camp, lay down their arms as a token of submission. If this is done, I shall order cessation of hostilities pending discussion of final terms of peace. Until this is done Her Majesty's troops will continue to advance." Upon further messages being received that the required arms and ammunition were scattered all over Zululand, Lord Chelmsford modified his demands to the handing over of the two guns taken at Isandhlwana, and all the king's cattle. Nothing came of these demands either.

A day's journey from the king's kraal, Lord Chelmsford formed a great laager and sent Buller ahead to pick a site for the impending battle with the impi reported to be gathering around Cetewayo. All that night, says Norris Newman, the chanting of war songs* could be heard from the hills around the camp. Next morning, July 4, at 5:15 A.M., Lord Chelmsford advanced in a hollow square containing 4,000 British infantry, 1,000 natives, twelve guns and two Gatlings, its front and flanks covered by Buller's horsemen and its rear by Col. Drury Lowe with the 17th Lancers. By 8 A.M. the square had reached the prearranged spot, rising ground 700 yards from the Nodwengu kraal, about a mile and a half west of Ulundi. Here the square halted and awaited the Zulu attack. Dark masses of

---

* Songs without words, waves of sound, rising and falling and "warlike in the extreme," as Colonel Durnford had written his mother.

Zulus were seen pouring down the surrounding hills. Archibald
Forbes describes the last great battle he witnessed as a war
correspondent:

Already there had been ringing out around the square
the rattle of the musketry fire of Redvers Buller's horsemen, as they faced and stung the ingathering impis that
had suddenly darkened the green face of the plain. A few
yards beyond the front stood the ruins of a mission station. The mouldering walls were ordered to be levelled,
lest they should obstruct the fire; and the sappers went to
work with a will. But there lay within those walls a
ghastly something that was not to be buried by the clay
crumbling under the pick-axe—the horribly mutilated
form of one of Buller's men, who had fallen in the reconnaissance of the day before. The mangled corpse was
lifted out; half a dozen men with spades dug a shallow
grave. The chaplain, who had donned his surplice, stood
by the head of the grave and read the burial service, to
which the shell fire of the artillery gave the stern re-
sponses, while the bullets whistled about the mourners.

The time had come. Buller's men, having done their
work, galloped back into the shelter of the square till their
time should come again. And lo! as they cleared the front,
a living concentric wave of Zulus was disclosed. On the
slope towards Ulundi the shells were crashing into the
black masses that were rushing forward to the encounter.
Into the hordes in front the Gatlings, with their measured
volleys, were raining pitiless showers of death. The guns
were firing steadily into the thickets of black forms showing on the left and rear. But those Zulus could die—ay,
they could dare and die with a valour and devotion unsur-
passed by the soldiery of any age or of any nationality.
They went down in numbers; but numbers stood up and
pressed swiftly and steadily on. The sharper din of our
musketry fire filled the intervals between the hoarse roar
of the cannon and the scream of the speeding shells. Still

the Zulus would not stay the whirlwind of their converging attack. They fired and rushed on, halting to fire again, and then rushing on time after time. There were those who had feared lest the sudden confront with the fierce Zulu rush should try the nerves of our beardless lads; but the British soldier was true to his manly traditions when he found himself in the open and saw his enemy face to face in the daylight. For half an hour the square stood grim and purposeful, steadfastly pouring the sleet of death from every face. There was scarce any sound of human speech, save the quiet injunctions of the officers—"Fire low, men; get your aim, no wildness!" On the little rise in the centre the surgeons were plying their duties, regardless of the bullets that whistled about them. The Zulus could not get to close quarters simply because of the sheer weight of our fire. The canister tore through them like a harrow through weeds; the rockets ravaged their zigzag path through the masses. One rush came within a few yards, but it was the last effort of the heroic Zulus. (This was the Umcityu regiment.) Their noble ardour could not endure in the face of the appliances of civilised warfare. They began to waver. The time for the cavalry had at last come. Lord Chelmsford caught the moment. Drury Lowe (Colonel, 17th. Lancers) was sitting on his charger, watching with ears and eyes intent for the word. It came at last tersely—"Off with you!" The infantrymen made a gap for the Lancers, and gave them, too, a cheer as they galloped out into the open—knees well into saddles, right hands with a firm grip of the lances down at the "engage." Drury Lowe collected his chestnut into a canter, and glancing over his shoulder gave the commands: "At a gallop: Front form troops!" and then "Front form line!" You may swear there was no dallying over these evolutions; just one pull to steady the cohesion, and then, with an eager quiver in the voice, "Now for it, my lads, charge!" The Zulus strove to gain the rough ground, but the Lancers were upon them and among them before they could clear the long grass of the plain. It did one good to see the glorious old "white arm" reassert once again its pristine prestige.

By 9:30 A.M. the Zulus were in precipitant flight. They lost 1,500 killed; the British, twelve killed and eighty-eight wounded. The shame of Isandhlwana was avenged, Lord Chelmsford vindicated. By the Zulus the battle was named "Ocwecweni," the battle of the "sheet iron fort"—the impenetrable square of flashing bayonets and storming volleys. Cetewayo watched the battle from a ridge about a mile away. When he saw his warriors waver and the cavalry charge out, he fled to the north, seeing from the distance the smoke of his burning kraal.

That night, learning that Lord Chelmsford did not intend to despatch a courier with the news of the victory until the following morning, Forbes, in his own words, hardened his heart and determined to go himself. Archibald Forbes's story of his night ride through the ruck of the defeated army is one of the great epics of war correspondence.

The distance to Landmanns Drift, where was the nearest telegraph office, was about one hundred miles; and the route lay through a hostile region, with no road save that made on the grass by our wagon wheels as the column had marched up. It was necessary to skirt the sites of recently burned Zulu kraals, the dwellers in which were likely to have resumed occupation. The dispersal of the Zulu army by the defeat of the morning made it all but certain that stragglers would be prowling in the bush through which lay the first part of my ride. Young Lysons offered to bet me even that I would not get through, and when I accepted, genially insisted that I should stake the money, since he did not expect to see me any more. It was somewhat gruesome work, that first stretch through the sullen gloom of the early night, as I groped my way through the rugged bush trying to keep the trail of the wagon wheels. I could see the dark figures of Zulus up against the blaze of the fires in the destroyed kraals to right and to left of my track, and their shouts came to me on the still night air. At length I altogether lost my way, and there was no resource but to halt until the moon should rise and show me my whereabouts. The longest twenty minutes I ever spent in my life was while sitting on my trembling horse in a little open glade of the bush, my hand on the butt of my revolver, waiting for the moon's rays to flash down into the hollow. At length they came; I discerned the right direction, and in half an hour more I was inside the reserve camp of Etonganeni imparting the tidings to a circle of eager listeners. The great danger was then past; it was a comparatively remote chance that I should meet with molestation during the rest of the journey, although Lieutenant Scott-Elliott and Corporal Cotter were cut up on the same track the same night. The exertion was prolonged and arduous, but the recompense was adequate. I had the good fortune to be thanked for the tidings I had brought by the General Commanding-in-Chief (Sir Garnet Wolseley) and by her Majesty's High Commissioner for British South Africa; and it was something for a correspondent to be proud of that it was his narrative of the combat and of the victory which Her Majesty's Ministers read to both Houses of Parliament, as the only intelligence which had been received up to date.

To his anger and chagrin, Forbes was denied the campaign medal he claimed for being the first to carry the news of the victory which had terminated the war.

The Zulus were defeated, Cetewayo a fugitive. A price was put on his head, and cavalry patrols scoured Zululand for him. His people remained loyal; they refused to disclose his hiding places. Some days after the battle he reached the kraal of his

[187]

chief induna, Umnyamana. From there he issued an order instructing his people to make peace with the victors. Cornelius Vijn, who was with him, says that he asked repeatedly what wrong he had committed to bring this ruin on himself and his people. After two weeks Cetewayo moved to the kraal of his brother Usiwedu, forty miles from Ulundi. From there he sent Umnyamana and Vijn to Wolseley with an instalment of cattle. Vijn returned with 500 cavalry to capture the king, but Cetewayo, warned of their approach, fled into the dark fastnesses of the great Ingome Forest, taking refuge in the kraal called Kwa Dwusa. Towards the end of August two parties of cavalry converged on the district, one commanded by Major Marter, the other by Lord Clifford.

Both commanders heard at the same time that Cetewayo was believed to be hiding at Kwa Dwusa, at the bottom of a steep valley. Lord Clifford decided to await the coming of morning. Marter led his men down the cliff. At 1:45 P.M. on August 27, his dragoons surrounded the kraal; the long chase was over. Cetewayo was carried in a mule cart to Sir Garnet Wolseley, who sent him to Cape Town. In the following year he was brought to England, where he was received by Queen Victoria and admonished by the Colonial Secretary.

The war to "bring Cetewayo to reason" was over, the "barbarian despot" a captive, his celibate man-slaying machine destroyed. It had cost the British taxpayer £5,000,000, and the lives of 977 Europeans had been lost. Four hundred and eighty-seven Natal natives had been killed, and an unknown number of Zulus slain. Countless more had been terribly wounded. The Zulu nation, in Shaka's prophetic words, had been trodden flat by the feet of a great white people.

Mehlokazulu, the son of Sirayo whose rash act had given Sir Bartle Frere the excuse he was looking for to invade Zululand, was identified amongst the captives. He was brought to Pietermaritzburg and handed over to the civil authorities for trial on the charge of abducting his father's two wives from Natal territory. He was taken before a magistrate, who, upon consulting the law books, announced after a lengthy deliberation that Mehlokazulu had committed no crime punishable by the laws of Natal. He could be punished only by the king of Zululand. Mehlokazulu was discharged "without a stain on his character," as the saying goes. Before he returned to his native land he told his "war story" to a reporter of the Natal *Witness*, by which it was published, the only "eyewitness" story of the war by a Zulu warrior.

16

INQUEST

THE SETTLEMENT OF ZULULAND was announced on September 1. Having drawn the Zulus' teeth, Britain had incurred moral responsibility for their future. There were two just and equitable ways by which the victors could dispose of the people they had wantonly attacked and vanquished: annexation to the British Crown or the restoration of Cetewayo, after extracting from him adequate guarantees of good behaviour. Either would have been welcomed by the Zulus, a people who respected British justice and reacted kindly to firm rule. But Britain did neither; Zululand was divided into thirteen parts, each ruled by a petty chief appointed by Sir Garnet Wolseley. He made a number of unfortunate choices; many of his nominees lacked authority and were chosen over the heads of the local tribal leaders who might have commanded the loyalty of their subjects. One was a Basuto who was given the job as a reward for his assistance in the war, another an Englishman, trader John Dunn, a man whom the Zulus had learned to mistrust. Over them was placed a British Resident who had little authority and no force to back up his "advice," once the British army had withdrawn to leave the Zulus to govern and fight amongst themselves.

On this settlement the London *Daily News* of October 30, 1879, commented, "The Ultimatum and its demands are things of the past. Rivers of blood have flowed to enforce these demands and now they are put on one side as utterly valueless with the settlement of Zululand and the release of Sirayo's son." The newspaper was not quite correct, for the chiefs were made to promise to disband the army, forbid the importation of guns and allow offenders a fair trial—promises that were impossible for the Zulus to keep.

The new order started well. The young men, freed of the burden of military service, hurried across the frontiers into Natal and the Transvaal to earn wages with which to purchase cattle and brides. Tribal councils met to judge offenders, ex-soldiers were ordered to give up the rifles they had seized at Isandhlwana, which they refused to do. But the new chiefs could not resist the temptation to pay off old scores; people were exploited, cattle were seized, men punished and driven from their lands. There was oppression, agitation, revolt and, before long, intertribal strife. Pitched battles were fought. Impis marched, slaying and plundering. Things went from bad to worse. The dispossessed notables urged the need for a strong central government, the restoration of Cetewayo. A group of chiefs journeyed to Pietermaritzburg to plead his case. The Superintendent of Native Affairs proclaimed that the peace of South Africa would be endangered if the rightful king of Zululand was kept from his throne. The captive ex-king agreed to all that was demanded of him; he would honour the terms of the ultimatum, keep the promises extracted from the thirteen petty chiefs. He would rule fairly and justly. He went even further; he agreed not to molest the women of the

Royal House, his erstwhile concubines, who had been given in marriage in his absence.

A new settlement was ordered. Zululand was divided into three parts; one part was given to Cetewayo, another was left in the charge of his cousin Usibebu, the strongest and most able of the "thirteen chiefs," and a third was made into a native reserve, ruled by a British commissioner, to which those who did not wish to live under Cetewayo or Usibebu could migrate. In January 1883 Cetewayo was landed on the coast. A troop of dragoons escorted him to his old capital. Once again Sir Theophilus Shepstone came to invest him with his royal dignity and to admonish him in his kingly duties. It was 1873 all over again. But with one difference: whereas at Cetewayo's first coronation the tribal chiefs and headmen crawled into his presence on their hands and knees, now they marched in upright. One even had the temerity to bring a European chair and sit on it in the royal presence. Cetewayo was uneasy; he spoke to Shepstone of his need to protect himself, of the necessity to rule firmly, to exact obedience, to kill if necessary. He hinted at the danger of assassination. With singular insight into British ways he complained that "should assassination be his fate, the British Government would do nothing beyond expressing regret and asking for information, and by the time information was forthcoming it would be found inconvenient to do anything in the matter, and so the assassin would go free, and his fate unavenged."

Shepstone and the troop of dragoons withdrew. The echo of Cetewayo's words of advice and warning had hardly died away when a fierce quarrel broke out between the Usutu party, the followers of Cetewayo, and the retainers of Usibebu. The pent-up jealousies and hatreds of the partition period were released; the Usutus sought revenge for the slights and insults incurred while their king was over the water. Led by Cetewayo's brother, Undabuko, an impi 5,000 strong descended on Usibebu's kraal; they met a crushing defeat. The two factions gathered their forces for the decisive battle.

When they heard of the civil war in Zululand, the Imperial Government in London were "much distressed." A dreadful threat was issued. Cetewayo was informed that if he continued to disregard his coronation promises, "it will become a serious question whether H. M. Government should not take the step of withdrawing the British Resident from him." While Cetewayo was digesting this remarkable communication, Usibebu, creeping up secretly, hurled his impi on the Ulundi kraal. Many of the Usutu notables were slain; a thousand huts went up in flames; once again Cetewayo was a fugitive, once again he viewed from afar the smoke of his burning kraal. He fled to the native reserve and placed himself under the protection of the British Commissioner. Then, on February 8, 1884, he died. Dr. Harvie Scott, the garrison surgeon, called in when the body was cold, and forbidden to make a post-mortem examination, pronounced the cause of death as "fatty disease of the heart." But rumour said that the king had been poisoned.

The Usutu party proclaimed Cetewayo's young son, Dinizulu, his successor. They knew they were not strong enough to prevail against Usibebu alone. Over the border the land-hungry Boers of the Transvaal, now once again independent of British rule, watched the situation. Sooner or later, they knew, one of the contending parties would call for their assistance. Long accustomed to take advantage of native strife, they descended like vultures on a sick ox. When the call of the Usutus came, the Boer government declared it "a Holy duty to accede to the appeals of the Zulu chiefs in the interest of humanity and civilisation." But before they moved in, Dinizulu's mark was secured on a piece of paper ceding land in return for Boer assistance.

A commando helped the Usutus to inflict a decisive defeat on Usibebu. His people were scattered, their chief a fugitive. Dinizulu reigned supreme. Then the Boers presented their bill; one-third of Zululand, 3,000,000 acres for their farms. All northern Zululand became the New Boer Republic, thousands of Zulus lost their land and became labourers on Boer farms. Dabulamanzi, the victor of Isandhlwana, was shot resisting arrest.

This was too much for the British government; they stepped in and annexed the remainder of Zululand to Natal. Dinizulu was deposed, the rule of the House of Zulu ended. In 1889, he was banished to St. Helena, but nine years later he was allowed to return to Zululand, being appointed the headman of a district. There he remained until 1906, when he became involved in a rebellion, upon which he was banished to the Transvaal, where he died in 1913. His grandson, Bhekizulu, was appointed Paramount Chief of the Zulu Clan in 1952—a title of authority which, though it carried no official status, was recognised by all Zulus.

The Zulu defeat in 1879 had brought the inevitable result. Within five months of the British victory at Ulundi, the Transvaal Boers, freed of the Zulu menace, cast off British rule. Four military disasters came in quick succession. The British government accepted Boer independence. The Boers were brought under British rule again in 1901, after the Great Boer War, and given self-government in 1906. Frere's dream of a united South Africa was achieved by the Act of Federation in 1909, by which black and white in South Africa were brought together under one government which became a member of the British Commonwealth of Nations. In that world-wide federation, the Union of South Africa remained until 1961, when they were forced out because of their policy of apartheid. Like all other South African coloured peoples the Zulus were subjected to the racial laws of the white conquerors, and designated as an "inferior race."

The Zulu nation had been trodden flatter than flat. As Frere predicted, they proved to be a people easily manageable if they were not brought up as wolves. They became lambs. Unfortunately for the Zulus, they were forced to live in a wolf's world. With the defeat of Zulu militarism went their only chance of survival as a nation or as anything but an "inferior race."

Lord Chelmsford, the conqueror of the Zulus, returned to England at once after Ulundi. His crowning victory failed to disperse completely the clouds that had gathered round his head after Isandhlwana, the disaster which the British public insisted on linking with his name. Disraeli refused to invite him to his country house at Hughenden. The Queen protested at his severity, but the Prime Minister refused to budge. He had nothing to say to Lord Chelmsford, he declared. The final years of Lord Chelmsford's life were uneventful. He made a speech in the House of Lords giving his version of Isandhlwana; he replied courteously to Archibald Forbes's stringent criticisms; he dealt sympathetically with Colonel Durnford's brother, expressing his desire to abstain from the bitter controversy over blame. He was made a Knight of the Grand Cross, an unusually high honour for an officer of his rank, and in 1884 he was promoted to lieutenant general, and appointed Lieutenant of the Tower of London. When the position fell vacant, the Queen made him her Gold Stick in Waiting: empty honours which then delighted the hearts of Britain's military caste. He died in 1905, aged eighty-one. History has been kind to Lord

Chelmsford. Isandhlwana is still officially listed as "poor Durnford's disaster."

Sir Bartle Frere was a ruined man. He was given no opportunity to retrieve his mistake. There was no Ulundi to wipe out the slur of Isandhlwana, to dispel the charge of "rashness" and "disobedience"; no seat in the Lords, no Gold Stick, no frolics in the royal bathroom. He was recalled from South Africa in May 1880. He had seen his policies reversed. He had taken a strong hand with the Zulus and adopted a conciliatory attitude to the Transvaal Boers. Sir Garnet Wolseley conciliated the Zulus and irritated the Boers. One satisfaction remained only to Frere. He had established the supremacy of the white race in South Africa. He destroyed the only native power capable of challenging it. In colonial opinion he had saved Natal from the horrors of invasion, rescued the Zulu people from the cruelties of their barbarian despot. The names of Frere's many Zulu victims are forgotten. He died in 1884, his South African policies discredited, his hopes for the reversal of the adverse judgment of cabinet and nation unfulfilled.

Frere, we might now say, was guilty of an atrocious crime against humanity, a crime to which, by default, the Imperial Government was an accessory: He had destroyed the Zulus, a people who had done the British no harm. Writing in the *Guardian* on December 10, 1879, James Green, the Dean of Pietermaritzburg, said this: "The Zulus never went to war with us, but we with them; they have always been excellent neighbours; for thirty years they have never been accused of stealing a sheep, or an ox, or a horse from the Natal side. Natal has no quarrel with them nor Cetewayo with us." Of Cetewayo himself Mr. Green declared: "He is a savage, and his ambition was to be a great savage; I do not mean a cruel one, but a powerful, influential savage. He was ambitious, but disliked progress, and such men must fall, so he has fallen with dignity. He has never attacked a neighbour white or black; he has defended his country bravely and has been guilty of no excesses. It has been our war, not his."

Mr. Green also gave his verdict on Frere: "Sir Bartle Frere says most truly that almost everyone he spoke to encouraged him to go to war; but I am afraid he avoided those who, he was told, were against war—and when will an Englishman not advise war? No argument was used, except the one that Cetewayo might overrun Natal at any moment; but he has never shown any deposition to do so." More recently a South African author, J. S. Marais, has said that the British High Commissioner "provoked a war against the Zulu."*

Because one is afraid of one's neighbour is no excuse for going to war with him. Nor is the good of the whole sufficient excuse for crushing a minority. Frere had the right ideas for South Africa. He wished to unify the white government and bring the natives under British control and protection. Unfortunately he carried them out in the wrong way. Even more tragically, having launched a war of aggression, he was not permitted to put the pieces together again. He wished to turn Zululand into a British protectorate, a "native state" on the lines of the successful British experiment in India, in which the Zulus could be weaned from savagery. He misjudged the Zulu menace and he miscalculated Boer resentment of British rule.

There is no evidence that the Zulus intended to invade Natal. Even if they thought they could achieve a sudden victory by surprise, they could hardly have believed they could get away with it for long. Cetewayo knew enough to realise

* "The Imposition and Nature of European Control," in *Bantu-Speaking Peoples of South Africa;* London, 1937.

that behind Natal lay a powerful nation, equipped with weapons which must in the end defeat his savage warriors. He needed to recall only the defeat of Dingaan by 400 armed Boers to recognise white superiority in battle. His orders to his impis, which were not obeyed, to avoid entrenched positions, and his refusal to allow them to invade Natal when he could have done so with impunity, demonstrates his desire to avoid war. He fought only when it was forced upon him.

The flimsiness of Frere's excuses for provoking the war is shown by his demand that Cetewayo disband his army. Zulu militarism could not be abolished by a word of command. The Zulu army could not cease to be in twenty days. Militarism could be abolished only by the destruction of the impis in war. Disbandment was no safeguard to Natal, for the impis could spring up again in a few days. Frere must have realised that; only by provoking a war could he secure the "self-preservation" for Natal which he so fervently believed to be necessary. The rash but, as it turned out, not illegal act of Sirayo's son provided him with his final excuse for crushing the monster which he believed to be so dangerous. Potentially dangerous it may have been. The situation could not go on as it was. Something had to be done to bring the Zulus and the British colonists "more in step," to use Cetewayo's own words.

It would not have been easy to help the Zulus adjust themselves to the changing world. It might have been done by negotiation and tact. But it was never tried. Frere was too impatient, too fearful of Cetewayo's young men, too anxious to achieve his ideal for South Africa, too much in a hurry, too eager, perhaps, to see himself as the sole arbiter of South Africa's destiny.

Frere's overeagerness to settle the Zulu problem upset the delicate equilibrium of South African power politics. The problem of the relationship of Boer and British was one that could not be decided in an afternoon. The British disaster at Isandhlwana ruined Frere and took from South Africa perhaps the only man who might have eventually reconciled the Boers and the British. Frere wanted to give back self-government to the Transvaal and keep the Boers within their own boundaries. If there had been no Isandhlwana he might have succeeded. If Lord Chelmsford had not blundered, the Zulu war could have been brought to a speedy and successful conclusion. Frere would then have been able to protect the Zulus and pacify the Boers. Because Lord Chelmsford failed to detect the Zulu impi lurking near his camp, the history of South Africa was changed.

Frere and Chelmsford may be the villains of the piece, the wretched Zulus their unfortunate victims; the true heroes of Isandhlwana and Rorke's Drift are the men of the 24th Regiment of Foot; they do not have to fear the verdict of history. In March 1914 Gen. Sir Reginald Hart, V.C., unveiled the "24th" obelisk at Isandhlwana, speaking these words: "The terrible disaster that overwhelmed the old 24th Regiment will always be remembered not so much as a disaster, but as an example of heroism like that of Leonidas and the three hundred Spartans who fell at the pass of Thermopylae." There can be no higher praise. The remarkable number of Victoria Crosses, eighteen in all, awarded during the Zulu campaign are evidence of British valour and courage. Significantly, eleven of them were given to the men who defended Rorke's Drift, the greatest number of national recognitions of courage, bravery and valour ever accorded for one occasion. Yet, curiously, this fact is not recognised or remarked upon in any of the books dealing with the Zulu war. The defence of Rorke's Drift is one of the greatest epics of British history; yet today it is strangely forgotten.

Let us close by quoting Disraeli's judgment on Isandhlwana. "A very remarkable people the Zulu," said Britain's Prime Minister in 1879; "they defeat our generals; they convert our bishops; they have settled the fate of a great European dynasty."

The first statement requires no further explanation. Bishop Colenso of Natal was excommunicated for his unorthodox ideas, his doubts about the validity of his religion being forced upon him by the enquiring minds of his Zulu friends. The death of the Prince Imperial brought to an end the Bonapartist claim to the throne of France.

INDEX

[203]

Zulu army, regiments (Cont.)
    cityu, 53, 73, 78, 91, 95, 185;
    Undi Corps, 34, 78, 108, 125,
    133; Uve, 92, 95
  tactics, 38–39, 41–42, 63, 77–78
  weapons, 3–4, 33, 90
Zululand, 4, 8, 9, 28–29, 41, 197
  invaded by Boers, 13
  invaded by British, 3, 15, 17, 27,

    39–40, 44–97, 109–20, 168–78,
    183–86
  partitioned and annexed, 190–94
Zulus, history of, 3, 6–7, 9–14, 15–
    16, 190–95
Zulu War, 4–5, 16, 17–27, 190–96,
    200
  major engagements, *see* Battles